No Mud, No Lotus

A Memoir of Sex, Betrayal, and Spiritual Awakening

Maya Yonika

To my mom
You are an inspiration to be who you are...
from whence you came.

To my Nana
Every visit to your house was the best day of my young life.

To my brother, Matthew
I miss you.

Table of Contents

Acknowledgements:

To Mom: for your love and acceptance of the material within these pages, and for housing me in between trips to Bali during my obsessive three-year writing phase. To Ben Jayston, for your endless encouragement, patience, and edits. Rupert Isaacson, for your straightforward advice and expertise. Daniel Wong, for your inspiration, ideas and support over the years. James Jim Catano, for your helpful advice and edits. Jennifer Summer-Fields, Vanese VaVoom, Gabriel Kundalini and Gillian Alexander for being my kickstarter cheering team! Laurence Huerer, for a stunning cover photo. And to all of my dear contributors, esp: Kecia Lipps Ruyan, Stephen Geiger, Richard Moore, Glenn Knight, Ocean Jucevic, Apollo Grace, Philip Ostrow, Roberta Candelaria, Jonathan Schell, RF Jonnson, Linda Kay Stevens, Chris Heaney, Alessia Lovino, Wayne Gowell, Martin Kirkwood, Martina Platzer, Matthew Marotta, Ted Scalise, Eric Vaughan, Dan Moren, Mina Gibb, Tanja Hams, Sonia Sanz, and Peng Wong. Thank you all for being the shining lights that helped birth this book into the world!

Although this is a true story, names and locations have been changed to protect identities.

The Guest House

This being human is a guesthouse
every morning a new arrival.
A joy, a depression, a meanness,
some momentary awareness comes
as an unexpected visitor.
Welcome and entertain them all!
Even if they're a crowd of sorrows,
who violently sweep your house
empty of its furniture,
still, treat each guest honorably.
He may be clearing you
out for some new delight.
The dark thought, the shame, the malice.
meet them at the door laughing,
and invite them in.
Be grateful for whoever comes,
because each has been sent
as a guide from beyond.

Jelaluddin Rumi

~Translation by Coleman Barks

Chapter 1 ~ Love's Conditionings

My name is Laurel. I'm eight years old, red corduroy-clad legs perched on the bottom rung of a wooden stool. My elbows are on my knees, chin in palms that frame these sad grey eyes that stare into a ten-gallon fish tank. Piscine shadows glide over neon-blue gravel. Water plants sway around a plastic castle, complete with churning water wheel and a tiny human skull that, every few moments, lifts to release a cascade of tiny bubbles.

A fat, calico goldfish with long and flowing fins waddles upward to smack its lips along the surface. Two vivid rainbow guppies dance in the endless spurts of a mating ritual.

When the female swims around the male, he tenses and curls his body, spreading fins and tail wide to quiver and flash like a peacock in the water. She turns to his left, but he darts ahead and cuts her off, flexing and twisting in his efforts to attract her, but again she turns away.

They play like this until she remains still, submissive, and then he swims gently beside her and turns his body ever so slightly to one side. A tiny fin protrudes from under his belly, and then, he lunges. She only stares at the plastic castle.

Weeks later, the female is fat- really fat - and with a bit of research, I diagnose her as pregnant. I haven't, as I first thought, severely over fed her.

Having never witnessed a birth, I keep one eye glued to that tank, and one day there she is, twisting micro-circles, and there, a baby fish sliding out! I think it's the head appearing, but actually, it's the baby's torso. It is a birth folded in half! And once out, in a matter of seconds, the tiny fish straightens and begins to swim towards the bottom.

Now giving birth to her second, the mother slowly turns towards the first baby fish, and to my utter surprise, in a flash she goes darting after it. But the baby is faster, and hides safely behind a plant, until the mother, turning in a half circle, again becomes preoccupied with birthing another. Out slides the second baby, folded the same way, but it doesn't straighten like the first: it's back is humped, suspended there, unable to move.

I jump up; scanning my room for a cup, a net- anything I might use to save the baby fish. Finding nothing, I grab a pencil and dip it into the water, trying to urge the baby to move, but the mother darts lightning fast around it, and snatches the baby into her mouth. My eyes wide, I watch her chew.

I live with my older brother of two years, my stepfather, and my mom, and I don't like a one of them. Mom stalks through the house in a perennial state of indignation: her tone harsh, her face drawn into a scowl. Never do I understand the source or configuration of her moods. I can't yet separate myself to see her plight with empathy. She is miserable, and I see myself at fault, for being me, for existing. We don't hug or talk about life. No discussions about girly things or feelings. We don't read books before bed, take trips, or participate in school events, and we move at regular junctures. I am an ugly duckling, an unfortunate mistake seemingly dropped onto a hostile planet... and I wonder why. My fish are my solace from it all.

•

"Laurel?"

I turn from the tank, to find my step-dad, Mark, standing at the door.

"Where did the money go?"

I look off to the side and scrunch my brow.

"What money?" I lift my hands and look back at him.

"Where is it!"

I search the floor for an answer. *Surely my brother's up to something again. Why do they even question me anymore? It's always him.*

"The money that was in your mother's purse, Laurel. Where did it go?"

"I have no idea," I say flatly and turn back to the fish tank.

He storms over, takes me by the arm, and pulls me onto my bed. He's got tape in his hands. He just tells me to sit down. I huff down and fold my arms.

He pulls out a piece of tape, rips it with his teeth and slaps it over my mouth.

I glare into his eyes. *Why? Why do people have kids if they hate them?*

He doesn't look back into mine. He only pulls out another piece, yanks my hands behind by back and wraps it tight around my wrists. Then he pulls another piece, this one even longer, and tapes my ankles together.

"I think this will help you remember," he says, and walks out.

I want so much to just pack my things and go. But, how...where would I go? Tears stream down the tape. My wrists hurt and I stay there for hours until Mark returns, peels off the tape and, calmer, tells me to go to bed.

No explanation. No apology. Nothing.

That night, I wake to a thunderstorm:

Before, I had told mom that storms really scare me, and she told me not to worry. She said, "That's just God, bowling in heaven." So, when the noise of thunder gets intense, I try to imagine God in his robes and a pair of black and white, patent leather bowling shoes.

Sometimes the ball rolls down the run, slips into a groove and peters out. But it's when he hits a strike that I'm most afraid, but I try really hard to be happy for him for making it. I close my eyes and imagine him throwing a triumphant fist into the air while the pins crash and thunder through the alley in the sky.

Lightning flashes and I open my eyes. My breath stops. The silhouette of a severed head is staring at me from the foot of my bed. Its hair protrudes wildly in every direction: a bloody horror, threatening to bite and to tear off my flesh.

My heart pounds and adrenaline courses through my veins as the dead head and I stare at each other through the darkness and thunder.

I close my eyes and pray. White light flashes through my lids. *Dear God, please. I know you're busy bowling, but I am so scared. Please, please make it go away!*

I squeeze my eyes closed harder. God has to answer this: I've never asked him for anything.

Another flash. I open my eyes. It's still there. Thunder again and I almost leave my skin. I sink into the down and cover my head with the blanket.

Minutes pass into hours, and the entire time I don't move an inch. But just as the morning birds first begin their song, I muster the courage to kick the thing off from under the covers. I take a few slow, silent breaths, jerk my foot, and feel the head roll off the bed.

Squealing, I shove myself against the headboard so I'm sitting up, yank the covers to my chin, and press my knees into my chest. There I sit, frozen again.

The morning light seeps through the corners of the shades, and my mom walks in. I'm pressed against the wall, eyes like a lemur, blankets taut in a death grip.

My mom looks at me and tilts her head.

"Laurel, you ok?"

I can't speak. I can't explain. She's about to see on my floor a dead head.

She looks down and reaches toward the head. A scream wants to burst from me, but I'm completely mute...nothing comes. She raises up with my favorite stuffed animal, Leo the Lion, dangling from her hands. Leo stares dumbly into the distance, his big, round paws swinging as she brings him over.

"Laurel, you're looking a little pale." She places him next to me on the bed.

I throw Leo across the room and collapse.

Chapter 2 ~ Toasty's Van

Swinging open the door of 'Lil Peach Convenience store, I swagger out into New England, dog-day heat. A chocolate brown van with fuzzy dice and a mini disco ball, hanging from the rearview, is parked in the lot. A grin sweeps over my face; it's Toasty's van. I'm fifteen, skin-tight jeans, black tank, and a blue bandana wrapped in a triangle around my neck. Peeking around the corner, I spy Toasty leaning against the side of the van, facing away from me. White stripes run along the sleeves of his emerald green tee, 'Toasty 69' in bold white letters, centered across his shoulders. Slinking behind him, I wrap my arms around his waist, startling him until he turns, and a toothy white grin usurps his baby brown face. A navy blue toothcomb juts from his afro.

"Hey, Toast!"

His black eyes shine; "Wuzzup, lil sis?"

We grab hold of each other's hands, slide palms to the fingertips, make fists, meet knuckles, hook middle fingers, slide to the tips, pull back exaggeratedly, make the sound of a pop, and beam at each other.

Toasty slides a cigarette from behind an ear, brings it to his lips, and I pull a lighter from my pocket to offer him a flame. Toasty pulls from his smoke, looks me up and down, leans into his van, and tosses a fresh pack of cigarettes out at me. I fumble, once, twice, finally catching it against my chest.

In an hour, he tells me, he's leaving to Woonsocket to meet a few friends. He's gonna go skating, then party at his friends. He tells me it's only a few hours drive.

"You want to come along?" He's got to work, so I'd be back by Monday.

I lean forward and peek into the side doors. The interior's covered in beige shag carpet, and a surprisingly tidy bed is built into one corner of the van. A poster of Jimi Hendrix in a purple disco shirt with an oversized collar hangs above the bed, a fat gold ring adorning every finger. He holds a joint while smoke billows in a thick ribbon from his sultry lips. Bob Marley is next to him with full dreads and a tender smile. Underneath, the text reads: 'Emancipate Yourself from Mental Slavery,'

"Yeah," I say. "Let's go."

Maple and oak rush past the van's window from where I lie in the back. The engine roars and Toasty's shuffling up front. I crane my neck, lifting my chin to see what he's up to. He's got one hand on the wheel, and with the other, is rolling a joint between his thumb and fingers before handing it back. *How does he do that?* Without a word I take it, admiring his roll.

I search my pockets, empty, and reach up.

"Light?"

Toasty presses a blue lighter into my palm. I stare at it- *How'd he get hold of my flame-* before I cup my hand and light the end. Pungent smoke slides down my throat, but I balk, and huffing the smoke out from my lungs. I always get paranoid when I'm stoned. I lift my hand to pass it back, but hesitate, and contemplate the joint again before returning it to my lips to take a quick second pull. This time the smoke travels further into my lungs before I exhale and slide my fingertips across Toasty's brown shoulder to pass it back.

Lying back, I light a cigarette and watch the trees go by. I imagine Toasty as a toddler, crawling around in diapers with his toothcomb stuck in his fro, waddling into his parents' stash to trip out on Legos and letter blocks. The van fills with smoke and my mind churns. Toasty puts on the radio louder than I'd like and I recognize the song: it's Motley Crue, but why do they sound more like the Chipmunks?

"What's up with the music?"

Toasty responds but I don't understand.

"Huh?" I ask.

He says something again, but I miss it and I feel awkward in my own skin and consider slinking under the bed covers to hide. But that would be weird, so I lay down to try and focus.

My thoughts drift to Michael. I wonder how he is; beautiful, brown eyed Michael. He was my first: just a few weeks ago, I was a virgin.

Before Michael, I'd dated a few guys, but that was a bad experience all around.

Andy was the last. He wasn't much my type: short, with dirty blond hair, crooked teeth and runty blue eyes. But he was popular and I wasn't...so I went out with him.

Andy brought me out to a movie and almost as soon as we sat down, his hands were groping my body like some slimy pig's snout busy in soil. He was working his way towards my inner thigh and I tried blocking him with the popcorn, but he'd snaked around it. Then I deflected his hand from my thigh with my other leg and pushed the soda in front of his face.

"Sip?" He shoved a tongue down my throat.

When I finally made it home, I practically flew out of the car, slamming the door behind me. Andy was smiling, waving as I walked around the car into my driveway, and I had to restrain myself from hocking a loogie at his windshield. Still, I figured, no big deal, it was over. But, that wasn't the case.

At lunch the next day, I'm sitting in the cafeteria across from Kim with the bug eyes, and a red tray with strawberry milk and a square of Friday pizza in front of me. I'm sipping through a bendy straw, studying the faces of the missing children on the carton while Kim's informing me that the strawberry is the milkshake flavor that gets infested with cow's blood.

I swallow.

My attention is pulled to the boys' table. There stands Andy, arms spread wide, in the center of the most popular and gorgeous guys in school.

He loudly proclaims: "She couldn't get horny if she did deep-knee bends in a cucumber patch!"

A burst of hysterics reverberates throughout the lunchroom. My eyes go wide. The boys laugh so hard that two of them drop and roll around on the floor. Kim covers her mouth and turns back to me, her eyes popping out even more than they always were.

I was a prude. They were right. I was shy, gangly and terrified of sex, and from what I could see in my compact mirror down there, there was no way a penis was going to fit in there. The only thing that seemed sure, was that it was going to hurt, a lot. Still, over the past few months,

I'd been thinking a lot about sex. I wanted to know what it felt like. I'd been eyeballing phallic vegetables and practicing making out with Leo the Lion.

●

I'm walking the hall between classes.

"Laurel!"

I wheel around. It's Michael. Drop dead gorgeous Michael. I look past him in search of the voice calling my name. Michael picks up his pace with his books tucked under an arm so he can catch up. I search his eyes for the joke and, finding none, turn to continue walking.

"Hi." he says.

"Hi." I say back.

I look askance, watching his feet in step with mine. A shy smile creeps over my face, but I'm still prepared for the punch line. He follows me to my locker and leans against it, watching me fumble with the combination.

"Would you...like to go to a movie this weekend?" Michael asks.

"What movie?" I ask, as if it matters.

"There's a Pink Floyd, Rocky Horror picture show double feature at the drive in," he tells me, "I have to look at the schedule to check out what time it's playing, but if you'd like to go, I'll give you a call and let you know when."

I look him over and I could swear he's being sincere, so I write down my number and hand it to him. He thanks me, and grins.

"I'll call you tonight!"

He turns to walk down the hall, folding the paper and tucking it into his back pocket.

I think I'm in shock.

That night, Michael calls and we talk for hours, and he's way kinder and sweet and real than I had expected. He'd like to pick me up Friday night to go to the drive-in. I agree, offering him directions. I hang up the phone and squeal, bouncing around like a locked up labrador that just heard: 'Wanna go for a walk?'

I pretend I'm watching the movie until Michael turns to speak with me. He's looking into my eyes and he touches my arm with his big, strong hands. I start to sweat. We're leaning toward each other close, and he smiles and turns, pointing at the screen. "Get ready!" He says.

Suddenly everyone in the parking lot is yelling, drinks and popcorn are flying through the air. A kid in speedos and sneakers runs over the hood of the car. The place has gone mad. Michaels pulled himself halfway out of his window: yelling and shaking up a soda bottle and the spray goes everywhere.

When everything settles down, Michael pulls himself back in and reaches over. He holds my face and kisses me, slow and gentle, our tongues meeting. He slides his hands down my neck, and feels my breasts through my clothes, then reaches under...I float into heaven. His touch feels amazing, and my insecurity melts into passion. His hands move over my thighs. I ache, his fingers run over my jeans, between my legs. I grab him by his collar.

"Can we take off your jeans?" My insecurity rushes back.

I look down and tell him I'm still a virgin, expecting he'll laugh. But he doesn't. Instead, he tells me he'd like to touch me, to use his hands, and assures me he'll be gentle.

I want him more than I've wanted anything, my passion a thousand times stronger than the fear, so I lift my hips, pulling my jeans down around my ankles, and open my legs for his touch. Fingers stroke the soft, dark hair, sliding down over my opening. I'm wet, very wet, and I don't know if it's normal, so I'm tentative and self-conscious. But Michael seems to be thoroughly enjoying all of this. He stays, barely moving his fingers over my clit, and I sink down into the seat, panting. The pleasure in his touch is excruciating. He slips one finger, then another inside, watching me squirm and buck, losing control. The more he gives, the more I want.

I pull off his shirt to discover his tan torso, beautiful and muscular. I pull his zipper down, shaking, afraid, curious, and reach into his boxers to ease out his cock. It's beautiful, and intimidating, big and hard- *how will that ever fit* - yet, his skin is so soft. I slide my fingers along his length, not knowing what to do, but he seems to love my touch.

I kiss his lips, imagining him inside of me, stroking him and finding my touch a bit awkward without some kind of lubricant, so I reach my hand down to my own wetness and apply it to him, discovering, to my delight, that he loves this.

I try going down on him like in a book I'd seen, but I'm not sure I'm doing it right because he pulls me up to kiss him more on the lips. It takes everything I've got not to make love to him then and there, but in the back of my mind, the thought remains that this is a once in a lifetime deal. I wanted it to be somewhere besides the middle of a drive-in.

That night when we manage to pull ourselves away from each other's touch and kisses, enough for Michael to bring me home, I climb the stairs and pull my clothes off to hop into the shower. My underwear and all the way through to my pants are completely drenched.

A week later, Michael and I are drunk at a party and he takes me by the hand and leads me up the stairs. He removes my shirt and my jeans, and sets a fresh towel onto the bed. I lay down on top of it and he lowers himself, watching me with his cheek rested on his palm, and asks me if I'm ready.

"Yes." I say, grinning impishly.

He stands and removes his shirt, then his jeans and boxers. I am in awe of his body, his muscles, the way he moves...the way his eyes follow me. We kiss, taking our time, and he slides his hand down my body, discovering I'm already wet and ready. His body is strong and beautiful, and the end of his cock slides along my opening. I feel every centimeter, every inch as he gently enters. My fingers tense as he moves, nails gripping the muscles of his shoulders, delicious as I feel him deep, but also intense, and in another moment too much. I slide my hand between us and he quiets, hard and still, while blood drips down my thighs.

It was done: all the mystery and fear, forever over and gone.

It's been several weeks and since then, and I haven't seen Michael, or gone home, or been back to school. I feel different, but I don't know why.

The engine roars, pulling me back in. I look into the rear-view to find Toasty's black eyes smiling back at me. I grin; shy that he might have somehow heard the story unfolding in my thoughts. I pull out a cigarette and light it, noticing the veil of stoned, heavy overwhelm finally lifting.

"*Shit!*" Toasty barks from the front.

A bag of weed, a bowl and rolling papers go rolling past me on the floor.

"*Hide those! Under the rug in the corner!*" Toasty says.

He's slowing down and rolling his window down fast. I look out the back windows, red and blue lights flash behind us.

"Shit!" I repeat.

Shaking myself into sobriety, I dive to the floor grabbing each piece and lift a section of rug that reveals a tiny cubby, puffing cigarette smoke around the van.

We're parked at the side of the road and cars race by, their speed forcing gusts of wind against the van. I look up to find smoke billowing from Toasty's window, and a state cop is marching up to Toasty's side, chest out, chin down, with a short-rimmed patrol hat pushed forward, over his brow. Tendrils of smoke disperse from his profile as he approaches Toasty's window. My forehead falls into my palm.

Toasty and the cop have a conversation I can't decipher. I sigh and fall back on the bed. All I can do is wait and suck on a cigarette.

The van's side door slides open and late afternoon sun floods in. I squint at a uniformed silhouette, demanding I step out of the vehicle .

"Ma'am."

I flick the butt of my cigarette just past his leg out the door, relieved that I don't actually hit him with it, and roll my eyes, sighing for the inconvenience. My heart quickens.

"No, we haven't been smoking, officer. No, we don't have any drugs. Yes. We're on our way to visit a friend. We're almost there, I think. No, I wouldn't lie to you officer."

He tells me to get back in the van, and he stalks back to his car, leaving Toasty and I standing in silence. I dumbly watch the red and blue of his lights flash and roll, flash and roll. A woman's voice murmurs in between the static pauses over the CB radio. Five minutes later the cop returns, and stands, legs wide, grounded before me.

"You said your name's Miss Laurel Yonika?"

"That's what I said."

I seethe, knowing my trip is over before it even began. He pauses and we watch each other for a good long moment until I divert my eyes.

"Ma'am, I cannot take custody of you as a minor seeing you are of age, but you should know you're a missing person...are you aware of that?"

My eyes widen and I nod side to side. *Fifteen is 'of age'?*

"Do you have someone you need to call?"

"I... guess," croaks out of me.

A wave of guilt twists my gut, squeezing out a distillate of delight. *My mom cared enough to report me missing?*

The officer leaves me, and patrols back to the front of the van. My mind spins and I fish for a fresh pack of cigarettes in my bag, trying to eavesdrop on the rest of their conversation. I light a smoke, set it in the ashtray, and lean forward, pinching the bridge of my nose. Papers shuffle, a seat belt clicks and the engine starts.

I pull my face from my hands and see the officer walking back to his car through the back window.

"What! Are you serious? He let us go?"

"Yeah."

Toasty flashes a highbrow glance through the rear-view to the police car behind us, then to me. I spy a naughty grin. He raises his arms to look around himself, as if to be sure he's fully intact. We roll back onto the highway and I sit back in amazement, questions swimming through my mind.

"I can't believe he let us go!" I say.

"I was one scared-shitless black man." Toasty says.

We both laugh. Ten minutes later, Toasty requests his gear and rolls another joint; this one he tucks behind an ear for later.

We pull into a roller rink in Woonsocket, RI. 'Highway Run' by Journey blares over the loudspeakers and we're enveloped in spotlights, the thick sound of skates on rink, and the bells and buzz of video games.

We swagger in, watching skaters making their rounds, and we search for Toasty's friends. Through the chaos, they're waving at us from the far corner of the rink.

"Dave!"

They clasp hands, and pull each other into back slapping bear hugs.

"Hey man! Long time."

Dave's a longhaired, hippie rock star, with a sharp nose and steely blue eyes. His lanky body swims in his baggy sweatpants, and a black, Thai-button sleeveless vest. His other friend is Chris. They greet each other the same way. Chris turns to meet me. He's a tall Asian with long black hair, full lips and panther-black eyes.

"Hi." I say.

"Hi." He says.

My knees almost buckle.

We lace our skates, and the boys are so eager they're tripping over each other to get onto the rink. I'd been on skates twice, so I tell them to go ahead. The boys are great skaters, and I watch them from a safe baby pace place by the wall. The skaters all move in an organic, flowing stream. They make it look so easy, crossing one leg over the other, turning to glide backwards, and then forward again. Spotlights play over the rink and a cool breeze brushes over my skin. Chris skates towards me. He flips around several times, and slows down to skate backwards and along side of me. He holds out his hands, inviting me. My heart's pounding, but I take them.

"Don't kill me." I request.

He smiles and guides me from the safety of the wall. Right then, the lights go dim. 'Couples time' is announced, and 'Stairway to Heaven' begins to play. The rink clears, save for the couples that are now joining together. My face turns crimson.

I fumble, arms flailing, and glom on to Chris, nearly pulling him down. But he halts and manages to steady my colt legs. It only takes a few times around and I'm standing straighter, and he encourages us to quicken when the song changes, and everyone piles back onto the rink.

Suddenly, I notice he's distracted and follow his gaze over my shoulder. Toasty and Dave are coming up quickly from behind. They're passing us now, Dave's long hair flying.

He looks over, cups his hands around his mouth and yells:

"Get a room!"

Toasty cracks up. Chris meets my eyes and steadies me. "I'll be back in just a minute," he says, nods as to affirm what he's said, and turns to bolt after them.

They glance back just in time to find an Asian rocket headed straight for them.

Toasty's eyes go wide.

He mouths, "Oh shit!" Arms flailing like a dancing crane.

Dave's already halfway across the rink.

The place turns into a whirlwind as they race, weaving with remarkable agility between the other skaters who are frantically clearing the rink. The three of them fly, tagging, pushing and pulling at each other, rough enough to move the other, gentle enough to stay up. Chris takes hold of Dave's coat sleeve and pulls him in a wide arc, passing around to his side, and Dave reciprocates the favor.

Toasty locks arms with Chris and the three of them sail in a wide semi-circle until, simultaneously, they let go and show off what moves they've got in the last few moments that remain. The music's been cut and only the thick sound of skates remains, and the inevitable voice of authority over the loudspeakers:

"Your attention: slow skating only. Boys, please clear the rink."

We're sitting at Chris' kitchen table with cards fanned before us. The game is appropriately named, "asshole." When you lose your hand, you take the shot of whatever's set before you. Tonight that means, tequila.

Chris and I sneak smiles and exchange shy glances. I lose way too many hands.

I find myself entangled on the couch, Chris on top of me, exploring with his tongue and lips. He's sensual and sexy and I really like his kissing.

But seemingly from nowhere, he stops, leans up and demands:

"Are you going to have sex with me or what?"

My stomach tightens. Bliss, in a matter of seconds, fades to black. I slide out from under him, telling him I'm not ready for that just yet. Chris gets up. His face looks disgusted, and he turns and walks away with a cold "Whatever." I shrink, suddenly cold, watching as he leaves the room.

Toasty. I get up on drunken legs to find him. I open a random door and take a few steps in, squinting my eyes into the dark;

"T?"

No voice responds, but the silhouette of a head lifts from a pillow. The long hair tells me its Dave. I'd forgotten about him, but it's a bed and I don't know where else to go.

"Dave, sorry to wake you up...I didn't know you were in here. Hey, I need to crash, is this ok?"

He lifts the blanket to invite me, and I lay down, grateful for a warm place to rest. I exhale the night of cigarettes, tequila and pot, and Dave's hand gropes beneath my shirt, squeezing my belly, roaming my breasts.

I freeze and his hand slides under my underwear, to my vagina. I don't fight. I don't move. I don't know why, I just go numb.

He pulls down my jeans. I hold my breath. His cock is inside me. The door flies open and light from the hall floods in behind the silhouette of Chris. He's yelling at us to get the fuck out of his house. I suddenly find energy to pull my pants up, gather my things, and rush past Chris in search of Toasty. I finally find him, sleeping, and nudge him awake, asking for the keys.

"Toasty, hey, can I sleep in the van?" *God damn it, why hadn't I done this in the first place*!

Toasty gets up in tightie-whities, fishes through his jeans, and hands the keys over.

"You ok?"

"I'm fine!"

I find the stairs and dash down them and toward the van as if I'm being chased by demons. I slide open the van door, slam it shut behind me, chuck the keys down, and throw myself into bed.

I lay there panting, waiting to hear the door to the house close behind Dave. I'll let him sleep here with me if he needs to.

But, there's nothing.

There's a hard knock on the van door. It startles me. I was just falling asleep.

Crawling to the door, I turn the handle and roll it open. It's the torso of a heavyset girl. My eyelids are so heavy I can't lift them to register her face. She says she wants a word with me. I stagger out, spying the ground to get footing and manage to look up to meet her. I catch a split second flash of a fist headed straight for my face. Somehow, as if I'm outside of my body, I watch the whole thing clearly.

The back of my head slams into the van with the shallow bang of skull meeting metal. I crumple, and am being pulled up by my hair only to be hit again on the side of my face. I fall, a heap, in the gutter.

"You don't fuck with Chris, bitch."

Apparently not- please, just don't spit on me.

When enough silence passes, I reach up to feel the back of my head. Nothing damp. *Thank God.*

I pull my face off the cement and look up. I catch a split second glimpse of Dave. He jerks himself back in from the upstairs window. *What a fucking pussy.*

It's morning. My head is pounding. One of my eyes doesn't open right. I lift myself from bed and crawl towards the front to look at myself in the rearview; the right side of my face is twice its normal size, black and blue, and my eye is swollen shut. *The elephant woman is in the rearview.* I flop back onto the bed, and doze off until I hear the door slide open. Toasty's telling me he has to go to work today, so...

I turn to face him. His eyes go wide and he jerks back.

"What the hell happened to you!"

"Long story." I sigh. "I'll explain on the way."

"*Some party, huh?*" I say, feeling the unnatural proportions of my face with my fingertips. Toasty's concerned eyes gaze into the rearview.

That day the sun's blazing, but I have to wait in the van while he's at work. I look awful. I'm not about to open the door, let alone go for a stroll through the park.

Perhaps Toasty told someone at his office, or maybe I was spotted through the van's windows, because a man comes knocking, offering a cup of water. I slide the door open and receive it, embarrassed. I know I reek of body odor and alcohol. Neither of us asks any questions.

Six hours later, Toasty comes back out.

The only place I had to go was home, but I hadn't been there in weeks.

Climbing the stairs, I'm trying to come up with some kind of excuse for my face. My mother's sitting at the kitchen table, chin resting on her palm. She sees me, goes white, and straightens, staring at me as I pass. I divert my eyes, rushing past,

"Where've *you* been?"

I murmur, "I fell up the stairs," bolt into my room, and slam the door shut behind me.

First thing I see is my birdcage. My heart sinks.

I have finches, three pairs: they're alive, but clearly in distress. They'd worked through their food and are diving their beaks through the empty seed shells in their dish. Their water is dark brown, almost empty and full of shit. I rush to their cage and get to work. I grab the box of birdseed, feed them, give them fresh water, change the paper, and finally collapse on my bed.

My mother. Why hadn't she fed them!

I'm dozing off when my phone rings. It's Michael.

Shit. I don't know what to say.

I pick up.

"Hi." I say.

"Hi," he says. "Are you okay? Um, where you been?"

"I don't know. I was just in Rhode Island a few days."

Silence fills the line.

Michael says, "I don't think we should see each other any more."

I tell him I'm happy to hear that because I feel the same way.

The line's silent again.

"Ok, Laurel. I'll see you around, I guess." I can hear he's upset.

"Yeah. See ya." I hang up.

My heart aches.

I go over to the cage, kneel and watch my birds. They are so tiny and sweet and dependent. I'd completely forgotten about them. One eye bruised shut, still hung over, my body exhausted, I drop my face into my palms. Tears stream through my fingers.

Chapter 3 ~ Alcoholics Anonymous

Obsession: A defense mechanism adapted in childhood to disassociate from the emotional pain we are experiencing.

"GOOD MORNING!"

A bitingly enthusiastic voice broadcasts over the radio, startling me awake.

"...And isn't it a BEAUTIFUL day to be ALIVE!"

I moan, peek at the clock- It's five a.m.- and cover over my head with the blanket.

My partner Brett bounds from bed, his arms are spread wide, shaking his hips while he chirps a zealous repetition of Zig Ziegler's inspirations.

"It's A Beeeaaauutiful Day!"

I roll into a cocoon at the corner of the bed.

When I first met Brett, initially I'd thought his motivational tapes and quirky jargon inspiring.

Initially.

We met a few months back in the program. I'm now nineteen and six months without a drink. He's twenty-nine, on his third year. With that much sobriety under his belt, I'm looking past the 'No relationships until a year sober rule'. He's sober enough for both of us.

It's actually my second sober relationship. The first began and ended last month.

A group of us were playing 'Truth or Dare,' when it's my significant other's turn to offer a truth.

"What is the most embarrassing thing you've ever done?"

He confesses that in his drinking days, he'd carved a hole into a baked ham...and fucked it. He even makes slurping noises with his tongue curled between his lips to describe the assault.

I know the point was to be vulnerable and admit our deepest secrets, and for the rest of us to simply listen, but still...the guy fucked a ham.

I really was willing to look past it, but that night when things were still fresh in my mind, he'd lifted me, naked onto his hips, and asked me to wrap my legs around his waist.

I was shy and awkward, but he was just having fun.

Before I knew what was happening, he was inside of me, ricocheting me up and down on his cock, like we're on a pogo stick. It was so blundering and graceless I couldn't even fake enjoyment.

I begged him to let me down, got dressed, apologized, and left.

Now with Brett, I hate to admit, things aren't much improved: he pumps away like a rabbit. Still, his innocence and enthusiasm for life is something I sorely lack, and this quaint cabin in the woods is at least a comfortable nest.

The coffee machine gurgles, sending a dense aroma wafting up the stairs.

Brett's rummaging down in the kitchen. *I should get up.*

I push my legs to dangle over the side of the bed, and heave my body upwards:

I feel like a walking comforter with a face.

Six months later, I'm in a sterile, cold church basement filled with alcoholics and their families, sitting in rows on foldable metal chairs.

The announcer calls out my name.

I rise and clamber over handbags and knees to get to the aisle, straighten out, and march towards the front of the room. It's a big day. My mother's at the front of the room, waiting to hand over my year sober chip. I roll my eyes, seeing the proud, goofy smile pasted onto her face. I've seen her once, at my high school graduation: it's not like she's had anything to do with any of this. Still, I'm glad she's here.

I walk up to her and muster a semi-smile. She hands me the chip and hugs me.

A rush of emotion courses through me.

You're in the center of a crowd. Hold it together.

"Let's go."

I pull my mom by the arm and turn to head back to our chairs.

My mom trots behind and the crowd cheers.

A month after I receive my chip, I'm sitting at a long table in the same church basement, my hands wrapped around a styrofoam cup of muddy coffee. An old-timer's repeating his mantra:

"My name's Ben, and I am an alcoholic."

I rub my forehead with my palm.

Some of the stories I've heard in these meetings are horrific.

Some guy's dad comes home drunk every weekend to beat his mom and he always tried to stop it. Once he got tossed aside hard enough to dislocate a shoulder. There was a guy here last week: his dad was the Vice-President of Montsanto. That kid was in seriously bad shape. One kid even came home to his mother, hanging dead in the kitchen. I just didn't have a story that entertaining.

My dad left.

My stepfather sucked.

My mom was miserable and angry and I kind of hate her guts.

My brother was sent away to foster care, and I hadn't even noticed.

Actually, I hadn't noticed that I hadn't noticed until now, really. I press the corner of my thumbnail to my teeth and bite into the skin. It starts to bleed, bringing me out of my thoughts.

I look up and recoil. Everyone's watching; it's my turn to speak. A streak of blood forms along the side of my nail.

"My name's Laurel and I'm an alcoholic." I hate that mantra.

"Welcome Laurel," everyone responds.

I pause, and lift my bloody thumb from where I was concealing it behind the table.

"I've bit my fingers like this since I can remember, even went hospital once because a finger got so infected they had to drain a massive pus bubble. You'd think that would have given me the incentive to stop. I tried, I even got this nail biting polish that tasted like death itself, but I gnawed right through the stuff."

I suck the blood from my thumb and realize I'm probably grossing everybody out and thrust my hands into my lap.

My eyes follow them following me.

"I'm like this with everything. The more I don't want to do it any more, the more I end up doing it...same with alcohol and drugs. What is it with that?"

I look up to blank stares.

"Ok, yeah, so I'm supposed to say what got me here."

"Two years ago, I was already using a lot and wanted to make something better of myself. I still do, actually. But anyway, since I had no money, and University wasn't an option, I got a credit card and enrolled myself in modeling school. I figured if my looks were what people wanted, I might as well get paid for it. Anyway, apparently my teacher at the school liked me, because after I graduated, she offered me a job." I look around the room. People sip coffee, watching me.

"It was a step in, so of course, I took the offer. It was really exciting, actually. There were big people doing big things, photographers and top pageant competitors and advertisers, everyone was beautiful if not famous, and I was a part of it."

"Anyway, after a few weeks, the girls at work invited me to go with them to the bars. I didn't think I could get in, I was only seventeen, but they instructed me to just walk in and act confident. Turned out they were right, and after a while, all the bouncers knew me and I could always get in."

"I really loved the bar scene. I felt wanted, and kind of privileged in there. The guys were fun and always buying me drinks. Plus, I thought it was really cool being my age and always getting in."

"But then there's that 'not knowing how to stop' thing. Every weekend I woke up in some random place, or sometimes in my own bed, but with no idea how I got there. I lived a good half-hour from the city, which meant people had driven me home. I gave them directions without even being conscious of it."

"I'd party on Friday nights and show up for work the next day, hung over and reeking, in the same clothes. I'd have the worst circles under my eyes, sometimes even hickies and bruises. The girls would take me aside and cover me with makeup."

"I remember on a Saturday, after one of those nights, picking up the phone. On the other end was a voice, deep and low, asking for me. He said he really enjoyed the night before and he wanted to see me again. Right then, a memory registered of the night before. I came out of a blackout just for a moment. I was being fucked. The memory startled me. On that morning, I'd left from an empty bed and didn't bother looking for anyone. I'd just run out of the house and looked for the nearest train station to get me to work. I didn't remember the guy's face. I wouldn't recognize him on the street."

"When I started gigs, the photographers would tell me I had to lose weight in my thighs. I wasn't overweight, most people told me I was too thin already, but still, when I modeled lingerie, the skin on my thighs would bump a bit when I wore tight elastic thigh-highs. So I started skipping meals and was pretty much living off of alcohol and cocaine. But then I'd obsess about food, so every day, I'd try to curb it by buying a bag of dried fruit to snack on, and kept it tucked into my desk drawer. But the fruit thing got weird."

"I was opening that desk drawer every second I had to grab fruit and chew like mad while staring out the glass door for students or clients that might be approaching. I was like a rabbit on crack. Another thing, there was this mirror. It was a massive mirror hanging on the door directly behind my desk. I'd jump up to look into that thing every chance I had, to fix my hair or my makeup. Really, I was embarrassed with myself. I mean, I'd sit down and three minutes later be at it again. It's when I started realizing I was seriously obsessive, and the more I wanted to stop, the more I'd end up doing it."

"Then one day I went on a mail run, and the world went sideways under the John Hancock. I lost all equilibrium. The office was right across the street, but I couldn't walk another inch. I just went down on my knees and sat on the pavement. All I could do was sit there and hold my head while people walked by. No one said a thing. I managed to feel through my purse for my phone and called one of the girls at the office to come and retrieve me."

I pause and look up. A few eyes are looking at me but most of them look bored to death. *Time to finish.*

"So... that's what got me here. Um, I've been a drunk since I ran away at 15. I black out every time I drink and I've been addicted to coke since the first time I tried it, and I'm really grateful to be sober today. Thanks for listening."

An awkward moment of quiet until I hear:

"Thank you, Laurel."

"Thank you," everyone says.

"Who wants to share next?"

A boy with wild blue eyes gazes up from under a black hoodie.

"My name is Max and I'm an alcoholic."

I fold my arms on the table and drop my head into them. I know this story like the back of my hand. Max gets drunk one night, drives his girlfriend home, he pushes the lighter in the dash and the next thing he knows, he's wrapped the car around a pole. When he looks over, the side door is crunched into his girlfriend's body, her head is tilted unnaturally backward and her mouth hangs open with blood trickling out. He barely got a scratch.

They were eighteen at the time.

I look up to watch Max. His hands shake as he pulls a cigarette from his pack, cups his hand around it, and lights it. He's so beautiful. I've seen him repeat this same story too many times. I wonder if he'll ever be able to let go of it. I rest my head back into my arms.

"Thank you Max," everyone says.

A month later, I'm pinching the thin rice paper of a joint in my fingers, passing the ribbon of smoke under my nose. I bring it to my lips, inhale and roll the familiar musk in my mouth, flirting with it, but I don't take it down into my lungs. My heart skips a beat and I pass it on.

Early morning, I'm staring into the darkness. I don't know where I am. Poison runs through my veins. I'm thirsty and the bed's wet. I turn my head to find someone sleeping there besides me.

My god, did we have sex? I close my eyes and try desperately to remember.

Chapter 4 ~ Colorado Dreamin'

It's late autumn. I'm behind the wheel of a shiny black and red flatbed Ford, my first real investment, ever. My boyfriend Michael is in his truck, just a bit ahead. It's a long stretch of highway from the East Coast to Colorado, our winter destination

Over the last six months, Michael's been getting me excited, painting pictures in my mind. His honey brown curls peak out from under the blue bandanna wrapped around his head. His sky-blue eyes beam when he tells his stories of forests and trails, hot springs, wooded cabins and snow-covered peaks. It was his idea to go to Steamboat and work on the mountain for ski passes.

Our trucks strain as we ascend into the Rocky Mountains. Maples and oak turn to aspens, blue pine and spruce. It's still warm enough though to open our windows and reach our hands out into the clean, fresh Colorado air.

"Howdy there lil' lady." Michael's voice chimes in on the walkie-talkie we'd bought for the drive.

"You might be interested to slow down a bit for them there elk standin' purdy due North roadside, cause if ya hit one of them things, your truck's as good as a tin can. That's a ten-four, ya hear."

Michael's brake light shines and I follow suit. He's waving and pointing through his windshield. I poke my head out the window and spot a herd of elk in the distance, just beginning to cross the opposite lane. The entire road's empty except one other car that's stopped behind them on the other side, and we slow and inch up to get a better look.

They're stunning; one male with a massive rack of antlers, and about eight or nine females. They walk slowly at first, then the male quickens his gait, and the others follow suit. Three of the females stop and look our way, their heads high, breathing mist into the cool air, before they continue, and the last disappears into the trees on the other side. Never before have I seen nature like this. Already I'm falling in love with Colorado.

When we roll into Steamboat, a shadow is slowly blanketing the town, as the sun sets behind the mountain. We find a curve in the road to park and step out to witness the last rays of light laid out upon the mountain. A handful of skiers fly down a run, passing a woman whose poles are thrust upward in a vertical V. She's squealing in delight or terror, we're not quite sure, and tottering from one leg to the other. Michael laughs, his eyes shining while he gazes at the mountain, and I look over to see the joy on his face, and fall in love with him all over again.

This is his dream and my first adventure living out of state. This is our new home, our new life. Our eyes meet and we beam at each other.

"Let's go find home," he says, and we pile back into our trucks.

Tomorrow, we'd head up the mountain to find work for the winter.

The snow's already thick on the mountain when we pile into the gondola for our first run. It's not a chairlift like I'm accustomed, but instead a suspended boxcar you sit in while your skis hang precipitously outside. A couple of middle age guys with snow weathered faces, dressed in board gear and jester hats introduce themselves: Marty and Jacob. They look like they must live in these mountains. I look out the window and pretend not to notice how Jacob's ice blue eyes are looking through me like a hawk. He pulls a joint from underneath his hat and licks the end with a twist, cups his hand and lights.

"Where you guys from?" He exhales a thick stream of smoke.

I let Michael do the talking.

The view from the gondola stretches far into the distance, valleys of aspen follow the rivers between lush, pine-covered mountains. Water bubbles trickle through crevices and stones in the icy streams that peek through melted patches of snow alongside of the run. As we draw closer towards the peak, the network of gondolas comes into view, and we enter onto a track that brings us through a small tunnel into the top of the gondola.

We pile out, grab our skis, wave our new friends adieu, and find a spot on the hill to click in. The slightest dust of snow is falling, and I catch clumps of snowflakes on the fur of my mitten.

I look up to catch Michael pushing off from the force of his poles over the lip of the hill, and effortlessly glide over the powders. But he stops just before disappearing around the bend, turning back and waves a pole, inviting me to follow. The snow is still barely touched, thick and inviting, and I start down. But as I make my way into deeper powder, I realize this is a completely different animal than the thin crusts of snow-covered ice I'm used to from the East coast. I'm struggling to maneuver, and try digging my heels in to plough, but I'm only gaining speed and going out of control. My body stiffens.

Damn, Michael's watching this- and bomb...straight for a tree.

My skis diverge in opposite directions. One twists, catches the snow, pops off, and glides on its own down the hill. I go rolling- snow, limbs and equipment flailing, until I land at the base of the tree, face down.

I lift my head, both traumatized and laughing. There's snow down my shirt and up my nose. I give myself a minute to feel if anything's broken, and relieved, roll over giggling, brushing the snow from my hair.

One ski still on, the other in Michael's hand as he climbs up sideways on his skis, gathering my hat and poles along the way. I sit up bewildered. Michael's laughing, impressed with my bail, asking if I'm ok. I assure him I am, and tell him I might take a while. I'd see him for lunch at the bottom.

He smiles, kisses my snowy face, tells me he'll check on me on the next run, and flies down until he disappears around the bend. Eventually, I make it to the bottom of the mountain, having made a decision to finally try what I've really wanted to do, anyways. I pop off my skis and head towards the rental store to trade them in for a snowboard.

Turns out, there's a lesson about to begin on the kiddie slope, so I strap in and hobble across the run, dragging the board awkwardly from my left foot. There are three kids waiting there. The two youngest ones, maybe five and six, must be brother and sister. They're stuffed into puffy down baby blue jackets with fur-lined hoods. The other is a lanky teenager with big black eyes and elvish hair that wisps towards his face.

"Hi'" I say to them.

"Hi." The younger kids return.

The teen smiles and looks at his boots.

I ask, "Know where the teacher is?"

The kids nod side to side, and the girl points toward the parking lot.

"But my dad's over there."

"I see." I say, already adoring them.

The elf shrugs his shoulders.

We look around for the teacher, and simultaneously crane our necks to watch someone boarding fast down the mountain. I recognize him as he comes closer; it's Jacob.

He flies in a wide arc in our direction, cuts the snow, and comes to a perfect halt in front of us. He raises his goggles to his forehead, and seeing me, cocks his head.

"You took a good spill up there, eh!"

I turn away, my face turning red.

"Ah- no worries," he says," everybody dumps. Maybe you'll like the board more, anyways."

He winks and looks to the kids, raising his hands in the air.

"Hey! You guys ready?"

The two younger kids yell, "Yeah!"

One of them is so excited, but strapped into the board, so bends his knees and stands there, pumping up and down. The elvish one stuffs his hands further into his pockets, and looks down with a shy smile.

Sliding down a hill on a single board without catching an edge seems impossible. I end up leaning my weight back instinctually when I start gaining any speed. Then the board goes willy-nilly and I either slam hard onto my face or my ass. Dumping seems much more violent than on skis. After an hour and a half, my body's stiff and sore, my ass is covered in bruises. But I keep trying.

Until the last dump: I go down so hard it feels like I was close to breaking my tailbone. I sit with my legs straight out in front of me, my feet still strapped into my board. Tears of frustration well in my eyes: my wrists, my ass, and legs...everything hurts. Jacob boards over to me and plops himself down.

"The first time's always rough with the board," he says, kindly.

I look at him, hopeful he's telling me the truth, that I'm not just an incapable idiot.

"So when you go next time, it's going to be easier. You need a little more speed and you'll be able to turn." He looks deeper into me.

"The most important thing to remember is to *lean into what scares you.*"

"You've got to brave this one," he says, "what you do on the board, you can do with the rest of your life. The sooner you move forward, the sooner the ride will become more fun."

Two days later I'm questioning my sanity while I watch the view from the gondola.

I clamp into my board and sit at the top of the hill, watching skiers and boarders start down the run, chanting Jacob's words; *"lean into what scares you."*

I stand, suck in breath, and push off on my heel-side.

I'm gaining speed way too fast, and the adrenaline rushes through my body. I want to lean back, but force my weight forward still pushing into my heels, then, wobbly, shaking, I'm about to catch the edge and bail...

Last minute I switch to toe side. *YES!*

I carve a wide arc, riding on my toes and that's a bit harder on my shins, so I come to a stop, satisfied with the leap, and watch a group of boarders fly past me, down the run.

The rest of the day I'm carving heel to toe in slow, wide arcs over powder all the way down. I'm still dumping, but every time I go back up, I straighten out and carve a little faster, with more confidence, heel to toe down the mountain. The freedom of the ride's so exhilarating and I'm doing something I thought was only for the privileged. It's been worth every moment of the pain and challenge.

And at the close of every day, satisfied, I park my board at the bottom of the hill to meet up with Michael and our new friends for shots at the bar. We party hard, go home to bed, and wake up in the morning with god-awful hangovers...but the mountain always beckons us to return and do it all over again.

Ski season came and went, and in the spring, Michael and I would cross a bridge, over a river called the Los Alamos, 'The River of Lost Souls', as we drove into our new home: Durango, Colorado.

It's a real live mid-Western town- Main Street's lined with bars, pool halls, and Native American souvenir and jewelry shops. There are Navaho and Zuni, silver and turquoise pieces in every window. In any restaurant, you can get a buffalo burger, steak fries, and a locally brewed beer on tap. I get a job at a pub that plays Country & Western and attracts the local cowboys and Indians.

Since I've been working nights, Michael and I barely see each other, and I haven't much taken notice. I'm at the pool hall in my time off, hanging out with new friends, namely Hippie and Jonathan. Hippie's the kind of guy I trust right away. His smile with oversized canines and his madman's giggle always entertains me, and we tell each other everything. Jonathan's green eyes and long brown hair gets the better of me upon first sighting. He's talented with his cue, and his love of the game gives me an excuse to rub elbows.

The story of another life in another town passes, and spring moves from summer, to fall, to winter.

And on a warm, sunny Sunday afternoon, Hippie walks into the bar, sits down next to me and casually inquires if I'd like to fly with him to Telluride. I sit there blinking at him.

"You're a pilot? All this time I've known you, and you've never thought to mention this?" Hippie shrugs. "Guess not."

An hour later we've packed a little Cessna plane with boards and equipment, and lift off from Durango's tiny runway. My belly drops on the bumpy ascension over the snowy mountain peaks with their wispy clouds, the engine loud in our four-seater cabin. My face is glued to the window watching the town shrink below. Hippie takes my hand and I turn to focus while he places it on the steering gear.

"Don't make any abrupt movements," he says, "just slow and gentle, feel the control of the plane."

"I... I don't *want* to control the plane!" I say, my hand suddenly stiff as I stare ahead.

"C'mon, Just play with my stick a little," he says, and giggles.

I shoot him a look and the corners of my mouth curl upward.

I push my hand forward just a bit, and the plane dips, quickening my pulse.

"Wheeeeee!" Hippie lifts his arms. I look at him, wide-eyed, grinning ear-to-ear, then back into the sky. He directs me to straighten back up. I do, with a little wobble, and relax into gliding above the clouds.

Once we reach closer to Telluride, the cloud cover grows thick. Hippie takes back the stick.

"I don't know if we can land here," he yells, "I'm not sure it's safe. What do you think? Should we give it a try?"

"What? What are you asking *me* for!"

We circle around a few times and he points out a hole between the clouds, and tells me to keep my eyes on it. I plaster myself to the window.

When we finally make our way through the clouds, Hippie lands the plane safely on the Telluride runway. I think I've never felt so cool as I do right now, unpacking gear from a plane before we head out to board Telluride Mountain.

Chapter 5 ~ Olman

On a chilly, hung over Saturday morning in bed, I hear a knock at the door. I throw the covers off, wriggle into a pair of Michael's boxers and slip on a tank. I open the door to Hippie, grinning at me with his hair dyed a god-awful bleached blond. I rub my eyes.

"It's early Hippie." I squint at him "What the hell did you do to your hair?"

"I got you a ticket to Costa Rica," he tells me.

My gaze drops to the papers in his hands. "You...what?"

I take the papers in disbelief, glaring at them.

"You have a passport and a bathing suit, ya? That's all you need."

Dazed, I look back up at him.

"Wait, Hippie, are you serious? You're bringing me to Costa Rica. Why? Nobody's ever bought me a present like this. I've never even been overseas."

"When you're a pilot, you get lots of good deals on flights, your ticket was pretty much free. What else are you going to do over winter vacation? Let's get outta Dodge."

I still can't believe he's doing this- for me!

I look at him deadpan. "Wait, are you in trouble, why is your hair blond?"

He giggles.

"The girls over there go crazy over blonds, all the guys have dark hair. I'm gonna get me some!" Hippie beams.

"Some?"

It's suddenly hitting me, this is really happening.

"Seriously, Hippie!"

I grab him and lock him in a bear hug and he pushes me away.

"Ewwww!" He smiles and winks before walking back down the drive.

"But wait. Hang on. Rent...my job!"

Hippie looks at me squarely.

"You work at a bar, just tell them you're going. It'll be there when you get back."

I look sideways. Where I come from, a job's a job. You can't just take off on vacations. That's when you get fired.

He turns back and points a finger,

"Get your stuff together. I'll see you Monday around five. We're on the red-eye."

Costa Rica is all I talk about at work, and people's questions remind me of how ignorant I truly am of my newfound destination. But Hippie was right, when I asked my boss for a few weeks off, he totally understands, no problem. Michael's the same. He likes Hippie. He's fine with me going. I'm pinching myself. People like me just don't get opportunities like this.

We land around 9 pm, drop our bags at a shady hotel, and an hour later we're at a disco. We're the only white people in the place. Black eyes follow us and we pass by a group of boys sitting along the floor that hiss at me like snakes.

I recoil, grab Hippie's arm and glare at him.

"That means they like you," Hippie explains.

"You're joking," I say, pressing myself closer to him, suddenly hoping to appear taken.

At first I'm wrapped a bit tight, but the Ticos are so beautiful and brown, healthy baby faces in knit hats with naked torsos, muscles and tattoos. Shots are being handed all around, and Hippie and I float into the crowd. Flashing lights reveal glimpses of bodies dancing and black-eyed glances. I find myself in the parking lot discovering I can get a gram of what tastes like really clean cocaine, for only about fifteen US.

I've completely lost track of Hippie until hours later on the dance floor when I find him parting the crowd, headed towards me. He doesn't say a word but just stands in front of me, hands on his hips, smiling. I stagger and smile back. Then he bends over and picks me off my feet, throwing me over his shoulder.

"Time to go," he says, "Wasn't that fun?"

I squeal, struggling to point back in the direction we came from, mumbling something about a cute, brown Tico boy.

Hippie and I pour over a map the next morning and take a few days to travel the tourist routes, getting our bearings. We end up hiking around deep into the jungle while the sun is going down. We're not quite sure where the path we're on is leading, but we've seen no one for hours. When darkness falls, we put on our headlamps and keep on in the dark, until Hippie douses his, and tells me to do the same. He points me to a spotlight just behind us, silently searching through the trees.

"Poachers."

He takes my arm and leads me a bit up a hill along the side of the road to lay flat in the bush.

A truck, silent and barely moving, rolls by.

When they're out of sight, Hippie puts his light on again and searches the land behind us. It's a flat open spot in the middle of nowhere.

"Let's set up camp here."

Suddenly we hear a low, dull growling and roar, coming from somewhere just ahead. It sounds like a pride of lions. My heart stops.

"What the hell is that?" I whisper in panic.

Hippie's quiet, listening to the sounds around us.

"Howlers." Hippie says.

"Howlers!" I repeat in a high-pitched squeal, "Oh my God!"

Just a few hours ago, one of the locals was telling us about howlers: very big monkeys. He warned us to be careful if they come around.

"Squat down and act submissive. Those things can rip your arms off!" he said.

"Hippie, what do we do?" I beg.

Roars echo, one after the other. The sound circumscribes us in every direction. My legs tremble.

"We set up camp and make a fire. They won't bother us."

I put my headlamp back on and a misty beam diffuses into the pitch-black jungle.

Ok, fire. I search my pockets for my lighter. Nothing.

"Hippie?"

"Yeah?"

"I can't find my lighter. Tell me you have one."

After a moment, Hippie presses a lighter into my hand. I look down, beaming my light on it.

"That's my blue lighter. How'd you get it?"

Another round of growls.

"Hippie?"

"Yeah?"

"Can we sleep in one tent tonight?"

"Yeah."

A foggy tinge of morning light softens onto the orange tent. Tropical birds, colorful singing, whooping and croaking fills the jungle. The tent walls drip moisture as I unzip the door to poke my head out into deep green plants, ferns and flowers.

I get up to make us coffee, unfolding a tiny Coleman stove. Hippie yawns and pops his head out of the tent.

"I'm sure glad them howlers didn't come. I might have had to throw you to them so they'd have enough to eat."

I light the stove.

"Actually, one did come, I didn't tell you?"

I open a mini plastic baggie of brown sugar and spoon it into a cup.

"And you know, she was the spitting image of your Momma."

Hippie smirks, nodding: "Bitch," he says, and slides out of the tent to find a patch of fern to pee.

I hear his zipper before he waddles over and kneels next to me.

"You sleep?" I ask, stirring our coffees.

"Really good, ya."

"Me too." I say, "so, where you think we are?"

Hippie grins, "I have no freaking idea."

"Seriously?"

"Seriously." Hippie says, groaning and stretching his hands over his head.

We pack and continue on the jungle path until it connects us with a quiet road. There is a massive bull in a small field along the roadside, reminding me of the kind of bull you see in nativity scenes: beautiful buckskin with long, floppy ears, a ring in its nose and a massive hump on its back.

But as we walk by, the thing starts to paw at the ground and throws its head. It looks really pissed and there's nothing between myself and it, but a single, thin wire, not a soul in sight. And it dawns on me: I'm wearing a bright red pack.

My breath stops and I swirl around to cover as much of the pack as possible with my body and try to pass, walking backwards, one arm wrapped around to the middle of my back to conceal what might be showing from the side as much as possible, the other arm over my head in an upside down L, to cover what's peeking over my shoulders. I crane my neck to look over at Hippie, who's wiping tears of laughter and shaking his head.

A jeep drives by and I sacrifice an arm to thrust a thumb exuberantly high.

The car pulls over. Hippie trots over as I mock him with a triumphant sneer.

Turns out we're half an hour's drive out of a little surfing town, so we drive in and find a spot to set our packs down and eat.

A little into breakfast, a girl walks in. She's cute, petite with round blue eyes and her long blond hair set in two braids over her shoulders.

She spots us, seeming relieved to find other tourists, and introduces herself right away. Her name is Mary. She's from Boulder, *what are the chances*, and she and Hippie hit it off right away.

They're talking about their interest in going to the volcano. Hippie had mentioned it earlier, and I wasn't feeling it so much, which led me to an interesting idea: what if they go together and play, while I take off on my own for a while? We all had phones, so it seemed reasonable enough. I brought it up and they were in agreement and the plan was made. I had my thumb, and I was ready for my first solo adventure into a new world!

That night, I end up on a beach somewhere on the South side. I've found a little bungalow to rent for a few nights on a tender grassy knoll overlooking the water, just above the sands. A massive orange moon rises up over the ocean horizon, casting a beam of golden light which sparkles over the waters.

In the chill of the morning, I step out of my bungalow, and the sand under my feet is already warm from the rising sun. Winds catch my sarong as I rest it onto the sand and lay down to drift into a dream.

I stir, and open my eyes to find a man squatting beside me. I pull myself up onto my elbows, startled. He introduces himself: 'Olman,' and sits next to me with a gentle smile to study the waves with his piercing green eyes.

He's in long shorts and an open turquoise and green vest with his black hair tucked behind his ears. He asks me where I'm from, if I'm ok, why I'm here alone. I'm wondering if it would be more appropriate of me to be offended by his introduction.

But I'm not, so I tell him. He listens intently. Then he looks at me and says he'd like to bring me a coconut.

He rises and I watch him walk down the beach to a small palm. He opens a knife from his pocket and holds it with his teeth, wraps his arms around the tree, and hoists himself, pressing between hands and feet, effortlessly up to the top.

Thunk. Thunk. Two green coconuts drop onto the sand.

Impressive.

He climbs down, and brings them to a tree stump close by, opening each one with a machete that seems to permanently live there, and walks toward me, a tan, muscular god with two coconuts in his hands kneeling before me with his offering.

Olman's the most relaxed person I've ever met. I don't know a thing about him, he doesn't say a word, he's quiet and contemplative, and when we're finished with our coconuts, he asks if he can see me tonight. I tell him yes, I'd like that, pointing to the bungalow across the sand. And then he's gone, leaving only his footprints in the sand.

I spend the day tumbling in the waves and then clean up to walk through an outside market close by. Fruits and vegetables are stacked high in weaved baskets. A heavy-set woman dressed in a gold patterned sarong and a head wrap smiles, showing a gold tooth while she trades blackberries and mangoes for my bills. The people here are so real and friendly and kind, there seems to be a depth and wisdom to them. I want to stay here. I want to live like this. I never want to go back.

I unpack bright green mangoes, lifting each one to my nose to take in their musk when I hear a knock at the door: it's Olman.

That night we walk until the first stars appear. I notice how intently Olman watches me, how he takes in everything around him. I assure myself it's not appropriate to feel love when I don't even know the guy. But there's an understanding, a familiarity about him that I can't explain.

On our way back, he tells me he has something for me. He winks and takes my hand, leading me to my bungalow. I sit on the bed and he sits next to me, pulling cloth from his bag, and lays it out on the bed, it's a bikini: amber, gold and brown. It's beautiful, tasteful and elegant. He signals for me to try it on:

It's stunning on my tan skin.

Delighted, I turn to him and model, albeit a bit shyly. He watches, waves his finger in a circle, directing me to show all sides. He stands before me and turns me around so my back is to him.

His hands are on my shoulders, sliding to the strings around my back.

He unties them, my heart thumps, but he keeps hold and unties the strings behind my neck, then meets them together, so my top remains on. He turns me to face him. I look down.

He's watching me, patiently. I don't know how to be in this calm silence, and automatically bring my hand back to release the strings from his hand. But he doesn't budge. He only traces my jaw line with his fingers and lifts my chin. He strokes my cheek and lips with his thumb.

He lifts me, lays me on the bed, and slides in next to me, resting his jaw on his palm.

I watch him watching me, and relax. I get the sense nothing has to happen; there is no feeling of *need* in him, no rush. I've never experienced a man like this.

Eyes glued to his, I reach to the center of my chest, and slowly remove my top. He takes me in, and reaches to the back of my neck to pull me forward, to devour my kiss. Currents course through me. I press my breasts into his chest, explore his lips and tongue; his mouth is natural and delicious. My fingers slide over the muscles of his chest and arms, nails raking into the muscles of his back, pulling him in.

He lays me back down, meeting my eyes, and bows his head to take my breast into his mouth. I watch him, his nose and lips tenderly brushing my chest and belly. He kisses and licks, moving down. My legs open, wanting his tongue, our breath deepens. His fingers slide down to my inner thigh, squeezing, then reaching over my bikini, running fingers over my sex. I push myself deeper into his touch, rubbing, teasing. He dips his fingers just under the line of my bikini. I want him.

He kisses deeper and slides his fingers under, feeling my lips, over my opening. I'm already drenched. Together, we moan. Slowly he rubs, electric, pulsing, dipping his fingers just slightly, without entering, driving me insane. I open my legs wider and buck, reaching to feel him hard against me and I hold him through his clothes, delighted how strong and beautiful he is, and reach under to wrap my hand around, finding wetness to tease and caress. I slide, gently stroking, squeezing... watching him fall into his bliss. He looks at me, smiling and licks his lips, gently pulling away from my grasp to push himself back. Rising, he pulls my bikini down over my legs, kissing the tops of my feet, and places my bottoms besides us on the bed. Watching me intently, like a cat, I smile and open my legs for him so he can see all of me, fully.

He is curious like a child, and explores my sex. The slightest touch from him sends me reeling and his fingers slide inside. I push into his fingers, deepening, aching, moaning. He watches my juices flow, sliding in and out of me, controlled. I'm losing my mind.

He crawls his body over me, taking my leg over his shoulder on the way, while he rises to kiss my lips, still sliding his fingers in and out of me. His lips move down my breasts, to my belly, to my sex, licking full, gentle, delicious, fingers sliding. My neck arches, I'm panting. I want him, all of him inside me, and I pull down his shorts, lifting my foot to help pull them off all the way, over his feet. We watch each other then, silent for a moment, but for the intensity of our breath. He climbs on top of me. I lift my leg over his shoulder, and slowly, gently, he enters.

We make love for hours that night, and when I climb atop him, he's holding my hips and gaze, rocking, us moving perfectly together with pleasure like ocean waves.

Hours later and still connected in our love, him holding me close as I lay on his chest...we drift quietly into sleep.

The remainder of my time in Costa Rica is spent with Olman. Hippie is off with Mary, and I trust he's well. I've turned my phone off and so lose track of dates and time. Deep down, I know, my flight came and went, but the idea of returning to the States leaves me empty and filled with dread. Still, I'm out of money with no plan or means, and reality is sinking in. I sit down next to Olman and explain what's happening, holding back a well of tears; I really want this to last. I don't want him to know the true mess that I am.

But Olman is kind and understands. He takes my hands in his and explains it's important I go back. He'll be here if a day comes when I want to return. He tells me to wait and leaves for a while, and returns with a jeep. He'll drive me to the airport.

I don't know what I'm going to do. I have no money for a return ticket. I half hope I'll have to stay. Olman brings me into the airport. The agents exchange glances as I tell them my story: I missed my flight. I have no money. I'm stranded. What happens with me now, is really up to them.

Amazingly, they ask nothing but a minimal tax, which Olman pays, and they hand me a ticket for tomorrow morning: my flight is at 8:20 am. Olman sets us up in a room for the night and we make love so sweetly, until the first of the morning birdsong.

On the ride to the airport, I'm prattling on about one of my favorite Costa Rican treats, 'mora', which means blackberry. I'm telling him how much I enjoyed Leche y Mora, Mora in the mornings with cream, Mora this, Mora that. I don't know what's come over me; I'm just excited about it. Olman smiles at me while wind whips through his jet-black hair, and he pulls his wallet from his back pocket. Driving with his elbow, he slides out his license and hands it over. I squint my eyes. *He wants me to see his picture*? Then I catch his name:

'Olman Mora.'

A week later, I'm standing in the bedroom, telling Michael I can't be in this relationship anymore, with tears soaking my cheeks. He's laying on the bed, one arm behind his head, the other pinching the crest of his nose, shaking his head.

"Why? What do you need? What went wrong?"

I can't stand to see him like this. He's been perfect, really. I don't know, perhaps since he'd gone after that girl at a party before we left for Colorado, maybe I'd shut him out then. I've never mentioned how much it bothered me to walk in on him leaning in to kiss her. Besides, a kiss shouldn't have been a big deal. I don't know what my problem is, why I'm so uptight. So I did my best to forget about it and go along with the program. And, we had our plans. But I'd crossed the line with Olman.

I tell Michael I don't know why, that I'm so sorry. I've got a bag packed and I'm heading out the door.

Jonathan and I move into a little trailer home his parents own on the outskirts of Durango. We practically live at the pool-hall, always playing shots for short chance, drinking pitchers and snorting cocaine. In town, we were the latest 'thing'.

But after just a few weeks of living together, I wake up to moaning in the middle of the night. I rush out of bed and peek into the living room. There's Johnny, sitting like a zombie, unaware that I'm there, staring blankly at pornography on the TV.

I'm hung over and my heart's pounding. I don't know what to do, so I turn around and go back to bed.

But I wake up to it again the next night. I walk out and stand at the door.

"Jonathan?"

He looks over, doesn't say a thing.

He gets up and turns off the TV and walks past me and goes back to bed.

It happens again the next night, and the next, and every night I wake to the sounds of moaning.

It lasts until the night I storm into the living room. On the TV screen, a man is fucking a woman hard from behind.

I scream: "What the hell are you doing?"

"What!" he yells back, "I just like watching it! What the fuck, I'm not hurting anyone!"

It hurts me. I don't know why, but fear courses through my veins every time I wake up to it. I don't know how to tell him that. Either way, I don't feel I am enough, so I'm over it. I'm done.

Chapter 6 ~ Delicious Extravagance

I'm at a house party on the outskirts of Durango, in a drunken conversation with a new friend, Sarah. Blond, pigtail curls bounce as she shakes her head. Her eyes squint out of crow's feet when she laughs.

I look up to find a tall, gorgeous surfer boy with long blond hair standing before me. A charming smile sweeps his face. He'd like to share something with me upstairs, and holds his hand out in invitation.

Sarah leers, and pushes her chin out, encouraging me to go ahead. I flash my eyes at her and tilt my head.

"I promise, you are going to love this. You're totally safe."

He whispers towards Sarah, "I'll take care of her. Seriously. Promise."

I find myself allowing him to take my hand.

He gestures to me to lead the way and follows me to the stairs.

It's dark at the top, and he takes my hand and leads me in through a door, opens it, and ushers me into a bathroom where a mirror is strategically balanced across the sink.

"My name's Leom," he says, pouring out a tiny baggie of white powder onto the mirror. He cuts four fat, precise lines with a credit card and fishes into his breast pocket for a bill that's already rolled into a straw. He tightens it up and hands it to me, curtly.

"My lady."

"Laurel," I say, grinning. I take the bill and bow towards the mirror, holding his gaze.

"Pleased to meet you." I say, before bringing the bill down.

I hold a nostril with my thumb, inhale from beginning to end, rise up fast, and grab at my face.

"OH GOD!"

My eyes widen. Tears well as a terrible burning grows within my sinuses. I shoot a bewildered look at him.

"It's ecstasy, a special kind, made especially for us," he says with a reassuring glance. "No worries. This is the best way to take it; it comes on fast. The burn will stop."

And he's right. As soon as the words are spoken, the burn eases and my perception shifts, I feel the chemicals moving through my veins, and a clean, relaxing warmth spreads from my core. I watch Leom: the lines of reality soften.

The world shakes into a blur...then stops. *Whoa.*

"Leom. The world. Just, wiggled."

It happens again.

"Things are going like this," I point my fingers up and shake fast.

"It'll stop in a bit. Your eyes are wiggling, happens to everyone."

"My eyes, wiggle?"

I look in the mirror. My image vibrates out of focus, until I'm there again. My eyes are wide and black, like an owl, intense. Leom stands next to me, the two of us, beautiful. My legs grow wobbly, a pattern on the tiles. I want to pee... *a release would feel so good,* I hear my name and look up.

Leom is smiling at me. I mirror his grin, needing to say nothing, but hear myself:

"God, I feel SO fucking good."

He takes my hand, and gestures towards the stairs to return to the party, walking in slow motion with me. I'm cautious, holding the rail: my motor skills aren't quite in order. His hand feels strong. His skin is warm. I'm shivering, not exactly cold, but I want to be covered in warmth and blankets. He leads me down the stairs. I admire his beauty, how he moves, then catch the buzz downstairs. Each voice melts into the crowd and back to solitary articulations. I try to return focus, taking hold of the railing, to make it safely down.

My breath deepens; being in my body feels delicious.

We make our way into the party. Distracted by my friends, I want to be close to them, and release myself from Leom's hand.

I join into a circle, noticing them noticing me. My heart pounds in my chest, still adjusting to the substance. Inhibitions are melting away and nothing remains but, yes, Love. They all look so beautiful it's overwhelming, If only everyone were to feel this. Still, it's clear we're in different dimensions.

I crave ambient music, warm, sensual and cozy...something sweet and juicy. But we're in a big, cold, ski house, drinking beer, with Led Zeppelin blaring.

My eyes start searching for Leom. His arms suddenly wrap around me from behind. I turn, meeting fire in his eyes.

"Would you like to meet some new friends?" I almost go to pieces in delight.

Every one of Leom's friends is stunning, including Rachel, apparently his girlfriend. I wonder if I should be disappointed. I'm not.

She smiles at me with shining grey eyes. I imagine how brave she must be to have Leom as a boyfriend, so I appreciate her right away. Some of the group's already making their way outside, it's clear everyone's privy to a plan. Rachel takes my arm.

"There's another party a few minutes from here," she says, "I think you'll be more comfortable there."

My eyes smile with hers.

We walk out into the cool evening air. I'm counting seven of us about to squeeze into a Volkswagen bug. I'm about to sit on a boy's lap I've never met, a Brad Pitt look alike.

"Well, hello,'" he says, offering his hand to help me onto his lap. I sit and have to crook my neck and hug the seat in front of me to fit in.

"Lincoln," he says.

I crook my neck further sideways to meet his eyes, giggling, and wrap my arm around to hold his arm in appreciation for giving me a seat. Hands are reaching all around while I get everyone's name.

Lincoln lights a cigarette, takes a drag and holds it up in offering. I inhale, meeting his eyes. I release a long stream of smoke out the window and turn again meet his gaze. His lips are thick and beautiful. I could kiss him here and now, I'm that comfortable.

We arrive at a house with a handful of people lounging on couches and beanbag chairs. Ambient music commands my attention: note and tone layer upon each other in details I'd never before detected. I find a comfortable seat, cover myself with a blanket, close my eyes and go deep into a colorful symphony of sound, pattern, and image.

Lincoln's voice chimes in, announcing that there's a game that's about to commence. I open my eyes and poke my head up. *How long have I been here?* We all look at each other, wide eyed and giggling in unanimous agreement, and make our way to the table.

Treats have been set out onto the table: candies, gum, clove cigarettes, juice and rum.

I sit across from Lincoln, meeting his eyes, and light a cigarette. He settles himself into his seat and signals towards the stereo, asking if I'd like to check through the music, try something new. His request caught me off guard. My senses are completely off. To navigate half way across a room to a stereo seems a major task.

But I get up and make my way over, kneel before it and blink, overwhelmed with buttons and knobs.

OK. First step: find CD.

I pick up a small pile. Psychedelic rainbow graphics pull me in.

I have no idea how long time passes before it dawns on me; I'm on task.

I can hardly read the names on the CDs, and flip through to decide via cover art, giggling at my ineptitude.

Lincoln shows up behind me, and pulls a CD from the stack in my hands.

"I bet you'll like this one," he says.

Gratefully I hand over the task and watch the miracle of hands in motion.

"I can't function," I tell him.

He presses play, helps me up, and wraps me around him. I'm awkward, shaky, my heart pounds against his chest.

But the warmth of him slowly, steadily quiets me.

I'm staring at three ladies and two Ace. This I can do. My game is on. All eyes follow the fan of cards I lay down before me.

Leom's lost just about every hand. He's sitting buck-naked and cross-armed, so just for him we're now resorting to dares.

I sit on the table and Trish pulls her chair back to get a good view of Leom turning cart wheels across the kitchen, wearing a yellow, floral print apron and oven mitts.

Lincoln's sung the entire Star Spangled Banner, in a nude headstand. We all join in on the song, Leom in his floral apron, me stiff in salute, and Trish waving her panties on the end of a broomstick.

Tyler, thin as a rail with long jet-black hair, who hasn't said a word all night, sits there with a cigarette and a shit-eating grin in polka-dotted underwear.

It's been a long night. The hours have passed quickly and we're all slowly coming down, buzzing and exhausted as the light of dawn peeks into the windows.

Time to call it quits.

Lincoln takes my hand, inviting me to sleep in his bed, and I'm suddenly questioning my want for his attention but it seems weird to just pull away after how close we've all been. Things feel different now and I wish I could just be home in my bed. but I'm here and I don't have a ride and there's not much I can do, so I go with him.

Lying down, I crawl under the covers, relieved to rest my head.

But I'm wired.

Lincoln slides in next to me, and I turn around to find a pink pill in his hand and a glass of water:

"It's Rohypnol," he says, "It'll help you sleep."

I take it, and few minutes later, I'm numb. Not long after, Lincoln is inside of me.

I disappeared for months into ecstasy, Lincoln, and my new group of friends. Every time I took it with them, my heart burst open. I'd never felt anything like it before: life was perfect and beautiful. Everyone around me was perfect and beautiful. My thoughts were perfect and beautiful. All of my fears and inhibitions, all of my problems just melted away. Ecstasy was the closest reference I had to love; what being alive was surely *meant* to feel like; pure joy, trust; simply bliss.

I remember the night when Lincoln told me about the heroin.

I was lying on a leather couch, watching a man fully animated, dancing on the wall. Lincoln kneels down next to me, amused with the marvel on my face while I glare at a Beatles poster.

He tells me that the ecstasy we've been taking is very special: from a master alchemist, a friend of theirs, his name's Mark, from San Antonio, Texas. He makes this stuff as a gift, especially for us. It's the most clean and pure ecstasy you can get, cut with heroin.

But then, something happened in the mix. The source went dry. So they said.

I wasn't prepared for that.

When a few weekends passed and I was repeatedly told the same thing, I turn from the doorstep of that house: the very place I'd been feeling so much love and openness, silently cursing, accusing them of holding it all for themselves. They were fucked up and greedy, every one of them.

The bars and pool halls become my hunting grounds. I drink more and do more coke. I seek more attention. I just want to feel good... feel love again. That feeling is my closest taste to enjoying life, to feeling happy and that I belong.

By then I'd figured out to buy large enough quantities of coke to sell three quarters at higher rates so I can do the rest. But it's not the same as ecstasy...not even close.

And regardless of being told it's over, I continue, in embarrassment even to myself, to return to the same door.

On my last attempt, Tyler greets me at the door, but it was a weird, zombie version of him. He invites me in.

The room is dark. Everyone looks dead. No music, no dancing, no hugs in greeting, they're all laid out.

Tyler calls me into the bathroom where he had a spoon with something in it and a needle, asking me if I'd want to try.

"Heroin?"

"Special K," Tyler says while he's tying a thick plastic band around his arm.

I can't decide if I'm fascinated or disgusted.

"Everyone's gone down the K-hole, it's cat tranquilizer. Same stuff they use to sedate tigers."

"Tiger tranquilizer, Christ."

I look away while Tyler sticks himself with a needle.

"Isn't this dangerous?"

My mind races back and forth, heart pumping, curious if I should.

But I don't. Instead, I turn and walk out.

•

I look in the mirror and stick out my tongue. My eyes are bloodshot and my face is bloated. I feel like shit. Who am I? Why am I here? I wake up lying in my own urine, with terrible hangovers. I don't want to do this anymore. Why can't I stop?

God, please help me to stop!

I need focus, discipline, meaning, and that arrow points up a pine-covered hill to Fort Lewis: an old Indian boarding school turned State University. I've ridden my bike up several times to walk around the courtyards and look at the panorama of mountains all around.

I have no money for school, but I have to find a way. I have to make something of my life.

I lock my bike, smooth out my shirt, suck in a deep breath, and walk in.

The administration office is all beige and bulletin boards, and a tall woman with thin lips and wire rim glasses greets me.

"What's your name, dear? Ok Miss Yoni- oh what an interesting name that is! What nationality is that? How do I say it again? Ok, Miss Yonika," she gestures for me to sit

"... You wait right there, I'll get you an advisor, ok?"

My heart's thumping in my chest.

Will they test me now? There's no way I can pass one of those tests. What if they find out I dropped out of high school for a year?

Questions race through my mind until the advisor shows up. She's a woman in her 50's, dressed in a blue suit with wavy brown hair. Her glasses are secured with a thin silver chain. She looks over her lenses with eyes in the first stages of cataracts.

"How can I help you, dear?"

She pulls out charts and brochures and lays them out on the desk. With the eraser of her pencil, she points out the steps I'll have to take to apply.

I chew on my nails listening to her words. I can get loans. I can get an education. Which means I can have real work, a real career, a real life.

The advisor stands up and I follow suit, *that's it? That was easy!*

She hands me a pile of applications and a brochure of courses to choose my classes for the coming semester. I ride back down the hill, beaming.

Chapter 7 ~ The Cave

I step, one leg then the other through the webbing of Ben's harness. He ties me in securely with ropes, and shows me how to hold the belay rope behind me and to the side with my right hand. My heart's pounding. I'm about to walk over a cliff edge.

I'm ready.

"OK, now lean into the harness and walk towards the edge. Feel how you are totally in control of the rope."

I nod, breathing fast, and allow the rope to slide through my hand until I'm standing right over the edge.

I look down. My feet are on the edge of a cliff and I'm wobbling above a forty-foot drop to the ground.

I gasp for breath, and pull the rope as taut as I can. My legs begin trembling, badly.

Peter is below me, looking up. A breeze touches my skin. My eyes dart to the tree beside me, Peter, the rock at my feet.

"Laurel, look at me. I'm right here."

I jerk my head up, meeting Ben's eyes. It's too late to turn back, and if I pass out, I'm dead.

"Ben, I'm so scared!"

I hate that my life is literally in my own hands.

"You can do this." Ben says.

He leans down his chin, holding my gaze, and pushes air with his hands.

"You are totally safe. Just move slowly, Laurel. Listen to me, trust the equipment"

"Ben, I'm scared!" I scream.

Tears well, blurring my vision.

Peter's voice chimes in from below. He tells me to keep my eyes on Ben. I do. My right arm is locked, frozen on the rope. My breath's erratic.

"Now, Let the rope out, just a tiny bit." Pete says, "getting over the edge is the hardest part, but you'll be more comfortable once you're over and parallel to the cliff face.   Try to sit into the harness, keep your feet on the rock, and start to let yourself down."

I jerk two inches down, and stop. Sweat, or a tear, falls down my cheek to the ground.

"Keep going," Peter says, "like you just did, little by little. You're doing great!"

I let myself go with another jerk, then another, gasping for air.

My body's parallel with the rock, legs straight out. Every muscle in my body is frozen stiff as a board.

It's more like sitting in the harness now. I take a few breaths. Peter was right.

"Ok." I squeak "Ok."

I release the rope more smoothly, sliding it in my gloves. Ever so slowly, I walk myself down the wall.

Five minutes later, covered in sweat, my feet touch ground.

I've met my match. Ben's all about pushing the boundaries of fear and limitation.

Ben and two of his friends, I don't know how, gained access to a locked cave, somewhere around Roswell, New Mexico. They told me I should go, this would be an adventure I'd never forget. But standing on this rock ledge, watching Ben turn a dial that secures the steel bars that block the entrance to a secret cave in space-alien-middle-of-nowhere-land, it's rather easy to estimate who's the likely candidate here for any sacrifice to the cave gods.

I'm wondering how I've acquired this inclination towards precarious situations.

Like an ant to a honey, a moth to a flame, a cop to a double- glaze, an altar boy to a porn site, a...

"Laurel"

"What?"

I look up.

Pete throws dusty elbow and kneepads my way, and directs me to put them on along with my hardhat and headlamp. Jeff takes three glass jars from his pack.

"What are those for?"

Jeff smiles, blue eyes shining, twirling a jar in front of his face.

"These ...are where we go pee."

I blink at him.

"What if we have to go number two?"

"Same. It's a virgin cave, can't leave a trace."

He unscrews each lid, takes out a roll of toilet paper, neatly folds several squares and places a package in each jar.

I go quiet, my mind busy with images of a number two circumstance.

The three of us take turns, crawling through the entrance into a spacious dark room that drops off into a ledge just a few feet ahead of us. Tiny bats hang from the ceiling; some are flittering about. Ben locks the gate behind us. My hand lifts and I suck in breath, about to ask if anyone else has the combination, but I close my mouth before it can come out. He ties a rope round a rock and tosses it over the ledge. It's a short belay to get to the base of the cave, and when we touch ground, Ben gathers his gear, and we stroll in a few feet until we're far out of the light from the entrance. We turn our headlamps off for a moment to get a feel for the world we're in.

Pure. Silent.

Five minutes in, the walls begin to tighten and the floor descends. Inch by inch, the ceiling sinks in, and we have to bend and stoop while we walk. I bump my hard-hat on the rock once, then again.

I can't easily follow them. I have to keep my eyes on the ceiling and pay more attention, or I could easily wipe out my headlamp.

The ceiling drops even more and we go down to our hands and knees and crawl. I'm thinking it'll be a moment before we're up again, but we just keep crawling. Minutes turn to a half hour and then an hour. Already a newfound kind of tiredness is working its way into my limbs.

Eventually, we come to an opening. It's a small hole of a room, and we all gratefully sit and twirl our wrists and stretch our legs and backs. I realize then, closing my eyes in the silence, there's a tangible difference in the air, no cell phone, radio waves, nothing. The emptiness is an extraordinary peace and calm.

I hear Peter giggling and open my eyes. He's huddled next to Jeff and Ben, headlamp in his teeth, while he pulls his blond locks back into a ponytail. He's beautiful, all blue eyes and muscle. He was my lover before Ben. We had an amazing sex life, especially on cocaine. He used to have me drenching towels. I don't know why or how it happened, but overnight my feelings changed, like radically, from what we had to a kind of repulsion. Even so, I'm happy it hasn't separated him from Ben.

Jeff and Ben are beaming their headlamps into Ben's hands. They've got a CD cover and are chopping something on it with a tiny pocketknife.

"What's that?" I ask.

"Window Pane" Ben says, shining his light under his chin so I see a reverse shadow of his face.

"Stick out your tongue little girl," extending a tiny black triangle towards my mouth.

"We're taking acid?"

"Yup. It's a gel-cap. Super clean. We'll be down here a while, you'll want this."

I've never tried liquid acid, but this is their domain.

I stick out my tongue. I'm not going to question it.

We walk for three minutes, and the walls go tight and the floor slopes downward and out of sight. I watch the boys turn into spider-men ahead of me, crawling with their backs pressed into the wall, elbows and knees against the other, shimmying themselves across.

I stand at the crevice dumbly:

"Um. Guys? Hang on, there's no ground."

Jeff turns and his light shines in my face and I squint.

"Shit ... sorry, hang on."

He scurries himself back towards me and reaches a hand out, coaxing me to stick myself to the wall with my pads like the rest of them.

I hoist myself up, stiff as a board, using every ounce of strength to push my knees and elbows into the wall in front of me. My gloved hands are clawing into rock. I'm panting. I want to get off this fucking rock. I shoot a look at Jeff next to me to see what to do next.

He's completely relaxed, the back of his head rested on the rock wall behind him. He lifts a hand and twists the beam on his headlamp low and rolls his head toward me. Green eyes look into mine. He lets his elbows down and sits back, using only his knees on the opposite wall to hold himself there. He bounces a bit for effect.

"See, this way you can just sit, you stick to the wall. You won't fall, just rest like this when you need to.'"

He plays around, showing me one arm and one leg holding him up, waving his free limbs exaggeratedly around until I break into a smile and figure out I can relax my death grip on the rock.

He got me going. I moved slowly, but I was doing it: Moving across a room with no ground to stand on.

I'm relieved when we find ground again. The walls suddenly open up to a massive room with giant pillars. I don't realize I'm tripping until I find the boys standing around a two-body thick stalactite. Suddenly I'm in some weird sci-fi alien show. The three of them all have their headlamps on, their faces only inches away, practically cross-eyed, as if they're observing something inside. I wish I had a camera.

I make my way over and my light is absorbed into a massive pillar of translucent, velvety amber. Veins of gold, red and orange, and ghostly rainbows run through it, as if it is a living, breathing, luminous, body. It looks so soft and warm, I can hardly believe it's rock and lift my hand to touch it, but as if reading my mind, Pete gently catches my arm, and looks at me sideways and winks.

"Only for the eyes," he says.

I'm mesmerized. But the boys have pulled themselves away, and are scampering through pillars that grow large enough to form walls. I join in, and we run through the space, separating, between them. Shadows scurry across walls in my peripheral. I look, only to shine my light into rock cracks and crevices. Another shadow flickers and whispers. Boots scurry, stirring up dirt that floats suspended in beams of light. Pete squeals and giggles. I shine my light his way and catch a glimpse of the scar that looks like a claw mark down the side of his cheek before he disappears into a cubbyhole. Gloved hands touch walls.

I look forward. Ben's standing there with his headlamp off, looking back at me. I lift my light above his head. His eyes shine red. Dust floats in the diffuse light between us. He lowers his chin, and grins.

Jeff darts out of nowhere, tackling Ben, wrapping his arms around him from the side. Ben yelps and Jeff bolts away, with Ben fast chasing after.

I stand there cracking up with the show. At the end of what must have been a quarter mile long room, we all converge. Ben's got what looks like a homemade map in front of him. He tells me I'll have to tuck into a room for a little bit: There's a place up ahead they might be going for a dive.

I'm relieved not to have to go further at the moment, so I'm ok with that.

Once they left, there I am, in a tiny room in a cave, tripping and alone. I turn out my light and sit in the dark, listening for the last sounds of the boys moving through the cave, until it is dead silent.

A cool breeze brushes over my skin and behind my neck, sending shivers down my spine. I realize I'm drenched in sweat. I turn on my light and my attention is pulled to the walls.

Surrounding me, from ceiling to wall, every inch of the room I'm in is composed of human skeletons, skulls, long bones, fingers, toes.

Ok, you're tripping, don't freak out, this isn't real.

I close my eyes for a moment to catch my bearings and my breath- *this is my test-* and open them again, to shine my light across skeletons, to look deeper in, rather than running away from them.

I want to look over my shoulder, to panic and jump up to see what monstrosity I'm sitting upon.

But I tell myself to breath and stay calm. I make a practice of it and turn my light out again. Somehow, surprising myself, I remain neutral and sit in silence, honoring the womb-like peace that is here if I choose to feel it.

I hear Pete's giggles again in the distance and sigh, made it. His head pops into the room and I look over, cool as a cucumber, keeping my light above him. He looks insane; his pupils so large that his blue eyes are now pitch black. Strands of hair float wildly from his head.

"Hey!" A giggle blurts out of him, "How ya doin?"

I giggle back. Tripping spelunkers are definitely their own unique kind of animal.

I've been chilly. Starting to move, I realize I'm stiff as a board.

"It's gonna hurt like hell the next few days." I say, stretching my elbows back.

My eyes slide to the walls and back at him. I'm about to inquire what he might see, but decide it's best to leave it.

"I'm good. Pooped. But this is worth it. Where to next?"

"Jeff thinks he knows where the keyhole is. That's really why we're here. Come on, this way."

He slips out of sight.

Keyhole?

Somehow we've managed to find ourselves crawling again. The boys stop when we come out to a fork. Jeff points ahead, asking me to lead the way. The room opens out wide and slopes upward, bottlenecking at the top.

Jeff points up the slope. I'm the smallest one, why don't I climb up and peek around the corner, and see if it might lead to another room? Otherwise, we'll go left here.

Cool, suddenly I'm part of the team, rather than just a tag-along. I crawl ahead, shimmying on my belly, and slink up a slope that, at it's tightest spot, veers to the right. When I reach the top, I can hardly maneuver my head. I point my headlamp into the darkness. Something moves. I whip my hand up, grab my headlamp and torque it to see what it is. Two massive eyes open up and stare at me. I heave myself around and slide fast on my belly back down.

What the hell!

My mind spins trying to grasp reason. *That* was no illusion.

That was: Two. Massive. Glowing. Eyes.

Nothing can live in here, and nothing alive has eyes like that.

Ben asks me if anything is there.

"No!" I say, my heart pounding.

I clear my throat to play down the squeak that just escaped.

I want nothing to do with further investigation into whatever that was.

"Nothing there. That's definitely not the way. Let's go left."

I don't think the boys noticed my panic, and I am distracted from it myself when Jeff starts clearing dirt from what looks like a wooden board he somehow found in the middle of nowhere. The boys are making excited noises. Jeff lifts the board and dirt slides off. I can see why they call it a keyhole.

"This is it boys and girls!"

Pete squeals. Ben grins like a Cheshire cat.

I don't get it.

Jeff's light is beaming into a rather small hole in the rock. Jeff and Pete wriggle through, but Ben, halfway, gets stuck and panics. He's begun panting; his belly rises and falls fast. His belt is caught and I do my best to direct him to unbuckle his belt so I can pull it off from my end. His breath is so intense, he sounds like a drowning man. I manage to yank the belt from under him and he wriggles the rest of the way through. I realize I'm shaking for him.

All of us in, we turn and shine our lights into a massive room.

My jaw falls.

Every inch, ceiling to wall, is covered in crystal.

Anywhere the beams of our headlamps touch is pure white snowballs of sparkling crystal masses, merging with translucent blue and amber, jutting in every direction. The boys are ahead, lights beaming from their third eyes like caving Buddhas, circling with their eyes glued to the ceiling.

We're in a real-life enormous sparkling fairyland crystal cathedral.

Pete is holding his head as if it might pop off. I've never seen a place so clean, so untouched and pure. *This is the kind of place where people come to gather crystals and sell them? I can't imagine doing so; it would be a rape of the Earth, a violation.*

I don't know how long we were in there, but at some point we wiggled out of the keyhole, replaced the board and covered it.

The magic holds us all in awe and silence until we are twenty minutes into the hour long crawl back, and we hear Pete moaning.

By then we'd earned our stripes enough to vent, and allow ourselves to join in the choir of agony.

That keeps us laughing until all of us, stiff, aching and sore beyond comprehension, take minutes to de-crumple ourselves when the ceiling finally lifts and we can once again enjoy the glory of standing. Ben looks at his watch and informs us we've been climbing around in there for fourteen hours. I do a double take.

When we finally make it outside, it's three am. I've never been so tired in my life. I'm not the only one to fall to my knees and crawl when the car's in sight.

That was my first caving experience.

Chapter 8 ~ The Road to Sobriety

It's my first semester of University. I saunter into the school store to fill my pack with all the books listed on my syllabus, and proudly bring them home to lay them out before me on my bed.

I stay clean that first week, imagining myself to be disciplined and inspired; pen tucked behind an ear, glasses on, hand gripped onto my forehead, absorbed in my studies in library corners and coffee-shops.

Once the novelty of getting in wears off, I go out with my new friends when I have a free weekend. This town is always going, and when I do have class the following day, I promise myself I'll leave the party early. But the hours always pass so fast, and I end up running home to shower in time to make it to class in the mornings.

Over spring break, Ben and I plan a cross-country trip to meet his mom and step-dad in Big Sur. We figure a straight shot's the best, so we pop a tab for the ride.

By the time we get there, it's three in the morning. We're still tripping when we pull into his mom's driveway. I tell him I'll be sleeping in the car. Ben tells me it's ok to show up like this.

"There's no f-ing way I'm meeting your mom for the first time, tripping."

But there she is, popping her head out the door. She steps out, dressed in a pink bathrobe. She's clasping her hands together; clearly delighted we're here.

"Oh my God," I watch her from behind the windshield.

She comes toward my side of the car and I busy myself, picking up trash, gathering my bags.

I look up.

She's right by the car, grinning ear to ear.

"Oh, how pretty your eyes are!" she says, "My goodness! Let me see... What color are they dear?"

This can't be happening.

I'm staring into the face of H.R. Giger. I can only imagine how wide my pupils are.

"Black and red!" Ben squeals, giggling.

My eyes widen and I crack up, turning to face him.

Her name is Rose.

She ushers us in and her and Ben take some time together while I jump into the shower.

Closing my eyes, warm water rushes over my head and shoulders, massaging my muscles. I settle in.

The shower curtain slides open a few inches. Rose is standing there, asking if I'd like a drink to help me sleep.

"Um, well, okay, that would be nice, what do you have?"

"Vodka," she says.

"How about a screwdriver, please?"

Minutes later, Rose's hand pops through the curtain with a screwdriver, maraschino cherry and all.

"Here you are, dear," she says.

I receive the glass, dumbfounded.

"Uh, thanks." I say.

Is this woman for real?

I dry off and hear a piano downstairs. Following the sound, I find Rose and Ben sitting together behind the piano, mother and son, he's playing the keys with her while she sings ol' rag time. There's a wide scar at the base of her neck, and another peeking from the soft curve of her robe. Years of pain, suffering and tenderness well over in her eyes as she sings. I stand and watch until they finish, and clap heartily, wiping away my own tears from the close of their song.

Rose and Ben get up from the piano.

"Well, off to bed," Rose says, clasping her hands and shrugging her shoulders before turning to hug Ben. She leans back, takes hold of his arms, and proudly looks him over.

"I love my baby Boy." She says.

I walk over and they both turn to me. I wrap my arms around her.

"I really love your son." I whisper in her ear.

We sleep in the next morning, foggy from the night, but the smell of coffee and pancakes wafting up the stairs pulls us out of bed. I can see Ben's step-dad, Mark, sitting at the kitchen table on the way down. He's massive.

 I follow Ben in.

"You must be Mark."

"Mornin'," he says, with a grunt and a nod.

He picks up a white cotton napkin from his lap, wipes his brow, chin and hands, and signals for us to sit. The table's set with a stack of pancakes, syrup, scrambled eggs and sausage. Mark wipes a piece of sausage in the syrup and invites us to dig in. Ben and I talk about school and Mark tells us humorous stories of victories in court. Rose tells me he's one of the top lawyers in the States. I try my best to pretend I'm impressed.

That afternoon, Rose shepherded me into her favorite boutiques, holding fabrics up to my face to get a handle on the right colors for me.

Over dinner, the waiter, dressed in tails, arrives at our table.

Mark introduces us, tells him "tonight we're treating the kids," and winks.

Appetizers: steak tartare, pate de fois ggras, caviar, and bruschetta.

Main course: a round of Caesar salads,

and for dinner: seared swordfish, tenderloin, potato and grilled vegetables.

He tells the waiter to bring his finest red.

I'm so full I can barely finish the salad.

While we finish off our wine, Mark calls over the waiter. He likes the wine so much, he'd like a case prepared to bring home with us.

The next morning on the ride home, I look out the window and watch the world pass while Ben drives. The angora scarf Rose bought me, undoubtedly the most expensive piece of fabric I've ever seen, is wrapped snugly around my neck.

With Ben's parents, for the first time, luxury and extravagance are in my grasp.

A year and some months later, it's a Saturday night in our favorite bar. I'm chatting in a circle with a few girlfriends and look up to find Ben standing on the bar.

"Oh shit..."

I cover my face with my palm and nod towards Ben.

"Look who's up on the bar."

He's done this before, a couple lines and some music that hits him, and he's on the bar flinging his clothes into the crowd.

An announcement is being made over the loudspeaker. Thud, thud, thud...

"Attention ... attention everyone."

Ben spots me and holds out his hands, inviting me to join him. I shake my head. I'm way too drunk to dance on a bar, but he doesn't let it go so I roll my eyes and file through the crowd so I can get him down. Instead, a bunch of hands are suddenly hoisting me up and I'm standing there, drunk, and the center of attention. The music stops.

I stop breathing, something's wrong.

Ben takes my hand

Oh my God!

He kneels before me, confessing his love, and then and there asks:

Will I marry him?

Now that we're wearing rings symbolic of stability and love, it's our mutual cue:

It's time to quit with so much partying and drugs. Ben finds a psychotherapist in town and we scheduled an appointment.

The therapist does nothing for me. She's got me holding a plastic baby doll and tells me to talk about what it was like for me as a child. I set the doll down, look at her deadpan, and tell her...it sucked.

I want to talk about what's going on right now with Ben. He just bought a ticket to England. He's planning on staying with an old girlfriend, Nina, for a month. He tells me they are friends. I'm not convinced that's all it is.

Her responses have that stone cold glaze of middle class, well-educated, indifference.

"How can that woman possibly help?" I complain to Ben on the way back to the car, "she has no idea what we're going through, there's nothing in her eyes."

"What are you talking about? She's a professional!" Ben yelps, "This is what she does!"

I stop and stare at Ben.

"I know. Honey, it's just that she's never...it's not *real*. She's book-learned, not experienced."

Ben looks at me like I have three heads.

I sigh and tell him I'll give it a chance.

A few days later, I find an ad in the paper for help with addiction, an acupuncturist who offers service by donation: Cherri. I write down her number and make an appointment.

Two days later, I'm in Cherri's office. I've never had acupuncture before, probably because I hate needles. Cherry's a tiny woman with short brown hair and lots of kindness in her eyes. I trust her right away. Except, she's got needles.

"Where are you going to put those?" I ask, my eyes following the package she's got in her hand.

She looks up and smiles,

"In your ears." she says.

My eyebrows crinkle.

"My, ears?"

I try to be cool.

"Does it hurt?"

"You might feel a little pinch," she says, noticing my expression, "it's really not bad. It'll relax you. You'll like it."

She pulls a stool up next to me and tells me to breathe.

She's right; it's not that bad.

"Why are you putting them in my ear?" I ask.

She explains that there are places in the ear that are connected to my organs and my brain. I tell her it would be a good idea to put some extra needles in my brain spot.

She giggles and looks at me tenderly.

"I want you to come in twice a week, ok?"

I nod, and my chin trembles and my eyes are welling up. No woman has ever looked at me like that before.

She places a hand on my shoulder and tells me she's finished. I'll have to sit here for a few minutes. She'll be back. She has another person to attend to.

I tell her I'm not going anywhere ... I've got an earful of needles.

I brought Ben in the next week and he fell in love with her too. She had a way about her, always speaking with respect and care. Every time I saw her, I could feel what it was like to be clean, and God, I just wanted to feel that way all the time.

Neither of us was able to just stop cold turkey, but the days sober were stretching to weeks at a time. It was the greatest progress I'd made since AA 12 years prior.

But although we were each other's impetus to be sober, we were, nevertheless also each other's Achilles' heel.

One or the other of us would eventually suggest going out, or bring home drugs; we've been sticks in the mud, let's have some fun.

We'd try to make parameters and rules, but that seemed to make it worse. As soon as rules were laid out, we'd want to rebel against them.

•

It's Friday night and I'm being strong and staying home while Ben goes out. I'm more determined now, and really, I don't even want to go out.

I'm fine...at first.

But the minutes pass into hours and I'm getting distressed and anxious.

My mind spins. My stomach is in knots. I call Cherry. No one there, she can't be there twenty four-seven. I pace the house, but my anxiety gets so bad I can barely breath. I want to jump out of my skin. I'm going to explode. I moan and jump around and scream into a pillow until I just give up and wrap my arms around myself and crumble up into a ball on the floor. My pup Jack, my saving grace, licks my tears and stays with me while I breathe. I can't remember why I'm doing this, what's the point of being sober when it's an even worse hell?

I've done so well for weeks. Tonight is Sarah's birthday party. It's a warm summer's night. Ben is staying home while I go out, and I'm dressed for the occasion: sparkling pink platform boots that zip to the knee, a mini skirt and leather tie halter-top. We all start at the usual bars and then go to the party. I lie down on a couch and sip a champagne glass that someone hands me.

Suddenly I hear the sound of a car horn blaring, startling me awake.

I'm in the middle of a dark highway and headlights are headed straight at me.

I'm frozen.

Brakes squeal, and a car; horn blaring, swerves to my left, shaving my side. I don't make a sound. The car comes screaming to a halt, leaving black smoke and the smell of rubber. The driver's side door flies open and an enraged man gets out, gesturing wildly and shouting.

I stare at him, unable to interpret what's going on.

Another set of headlights on the opposite side of the road is coming. Shaking, I make my way to the side of the road.

'I'm...sorry.' I say. *Where the hell am I?*

The driver glares at me, seething, while I stand there shivering.

He shakes his head, throws himself into his seat, slams the door and squeals off.

I sit on the guardrail and try to gain my bearings. It's foggy, maybe three or four in the morning. Looking around, I begin to recognize where I am, on a main route not far from home.

My heart is pounding and my limbs are numb, *what the fuck just happened?*

I dig though my purse, shaking; thank god I have my phone. I pull it out and call Ben, praying to hear his voice. I just want to be home laying my body next to Ben. The phone is ringing, I run home with the phone to my ear. *Please, please answer Ben!*

Ben brings me to the hospital that night, reasoning that we'd better make sure I wasn't raped. I hate the idea but I'm a mess and it's true I have no idea what happened. When we get to the waiting room, it's five in the morning, and we wait an hour until the doctor arrives. When the doctor walks in, he pushes his chin down and looks me up and down over his glasses. Shaking his head, he flips through his papers.

"Miss Yonika," he states, then shoots me a look and returns to his papers, "what is it, exactly, that I can do for you?"

I get up.

"Nothing." I seethe through my teeth.

"I don't need anything." I say, and storm out.

Ben is in England with Nina. It never got reconciled with the psychiatrist. Nothing, in fact, was getting resolved with that zombie bitch. Surely while my daddy was gone, off with his new wife happily making another family, hers was paying for her fine education so she could study up and tell me how to get by in the world. That made sense. Fuck that dumb bitch. Fuck everything. Ben, my fiance, is in another country for a month with another woman. He wanted to go be with her, so he went.

Finals are coming up and I'm doing my best to focus, but I've got so much anxiety I can hardly sit still. So when I go out to the bars and meet Richard, Ben isn't the first thing I mention.

After Ben returns, I confess to him that I've been spending time with Richard, and yes, I have some feelings for him, but I wanted Ben and I to work, so I haven't taken it anywhere serious, all I've done is kiss him. I was hoping the conversation would create some understanding, an opening into all that was going on, But instead, Ben grabs me by the arm, drags me naked off the bed. I go limp, bumping onto the floor.

Nothing is said after that, not about Nina or Richard, or much of anything, in fact. After that, Ben and I find ways to avoid each other. We've been together for two years, and this was the beginning of the end.

I go out a few more times to the bars in search of Richard, but the nights are cut short when my heart begins thumping out of control with intense murmurs, and my hangovers are more painful than I can handle. I can barely move. My face is bloated. My body can no longer handle this.

Ben is out with his friends. I pull off my ring, leaving it in a desk drawer, grab Jack and a bag of clothes, and leave with a man in a van headed for California.

Chapter 9 ~ Kali Awakening

Max and I travel together for two and a half weeks before we roll into California. He pulls along the roadside on Rt1 in Pacific Grove.

"This is Lover's Point." One side of his mouth curls up, and he pulls the shifter to park.

We hop out and walk over to sit at the top of a cliff, to watch the waves crash into the rocks below, rising ocean mists that cool our faces.

I've been his lover, albeit a kind of currency, as I have with so many others in my past: a means to get from point A to point B. I was honest with him that this was temporary, I'd be getting off the bus somewhere in California. But he has his own initiatives, hopes and expectations, and as with all elusive sexual agreements, the parameters eventually become ragged. Confusion and shadow seeps in.

But things are becoming even more complex than I might have expected, had I given reasonable contemplation to our circumstances. Through our travels, I've been becoming aware that Max has what appears to be a split personality, or perhaps some kind of psychosis or intense paranoia or something. Whatever it is, the closer we come to the California border, the more his 'other' self was making itself known. He's been telling me stories about secret information, and large sums of money buried on a piece of land in Utah. Soon we have to go and retrieve it. But there are people who know what he knows. They're after him: the people from the government. He talks about the CIA, LSD, mind control, code names, honey traps, and he looks at me really strange when he talks about honey traps. I think he's thinking I'm one of them.

This is no whimsical, new age confusion. This is straight up scary shit. I've been sleeping with this man, and I seriously have the creeps. But I've gotten myself into this situation. Now, I have to get myself out.

We continue driving south, through Santa Cruz and down Route Nine, an old red-light district road winding through thick forests of eucalyptus and redwood old growth, and land in a sleepy town called Felton. There we stop the van to go into a sweet little organic market that, to my astonishment, has 'Help Wanted,' posted on the entrance door. Max didn't notice, and I don't mention it, and after we unpack our groceries into coolers in the van, he tells me he's going for a walk,

I can barely contain my excitement. I wait until Max's out of sight and walk back into the market.

I ask the girl at the register if they might be seeking help in produce? I have a lot of experience.

She tells me to hang on and makes an announcement, calling the produce managers up, and only moments later, two men in their early fifties, one tall and lanky, and the other stocky with salt and pepper curls, come strolling down the aisle. Wide, friendly smiles on their faces, they offer their hands.

The tall one's Burt, and the other, Ernie.

My eyes roam from one to the other.

"You guys, serious?"

They look at each other, still grinning.

"Yup," Burt says with a nod, "that's our real names."

"How can we help you?" Ernie asks.

We all go to the back room and I tell them my experience and the story that's brought me here. I wonder if I'm insane to let them know I'm here to put my head down and work to get sober from a drug addiction. This is my first step. I don't even have a home here yet.

"I'm serious and dependable and really keen on working, and I saw your sign."

Then a miracle happens. They hire me on the spot.

The following day, when Max's outside sitting on a redwood stump and I'm making lunch, I get a call on my cell. It's Burt.

"There's a little cabin available just down the road from where you're parked. The man who lives there needs a roommate right away and guess what? He's been sober for two years. Would you be interested?"

He gives me directions and I hang up the phone, put Jack on his leash, tell Max his sandwich is on the counter, and go running to take a look.

The cabin's perched on a hillside with a deck above the river on a quiet country road, surrounded by lush ferns and redwood. It's perfect.

I tell Max I've found a place and I'm leaving in the morning, and to my relief, he takes the news well: too well, in fact. The way he's been behaving, I don't trust he's going to just let this go.

We sleep peacefully that night, and in the morning I hop up, excited and nervous, and gather my things. The house isn't far but I don't want Max to know where I'll be living.

"Thank you so much. I've really appreciated our journey together, and I'm ready to be on my own now. I don't need a ride, really, I want to walk."

I put Jack on his leash, grab my bags and hug Max goodbye. My shoulders drop when I turn the corner out of sight. It all went in stride.

Jack trots beside me, happy as a lark, with his tongue hanging out, looking up at me with his big brown eyes, as if he's questioning where this adventure's taking us now. When we get to the house, right away Jack bounds off to play with my new roommate Greg while I unpack my bags. They're already in love. Tomorrow is my first day in my new job.

Every day I wake with the sun to create colorful mandalas of stacked, fresh organic fruits and vegetables, just to tear it all down the next day and do it all over again.

Max showed up on my third day on the job. I'd omitted this detail of the story in my interview hoping it was done and I'd never see him again. But, apparently, he knew because he comes right up to my cart and slams down onto it what looks like a huge stack of money, wrapped tight in black plastic. I look down at it, and back at him. He's wearing a pair of dark, Robocop sunglasses.

"So, what's that about?" I ask.

"It's for you." Max says in a dead tone.

"I don't want it."

He stares at me through his glasses. I can't see his eyes, but I feel the burn.

"Max, you have to let me be. I'm working, and we're done."

Burt magically shows up out of nowhere and stands beside me. Max looks at me, then to Burt, sneers and shakes his head and walks behind us to head down the aisle towards the back of the store. What I don't yet know is, Max had a knuckle pressed stiff into Burt's back as he passed.

"That guy's dangerous." Burt says as we shuck corn together in the back room.

"He wanted it to feel like a gun.'"

Max comes in again the next day, this time with an empty aspirin bottle. He shakes it like a rattle and says found it on the floor of his van.

"So," I ask, "what's that got to do with me?"

What was I doing, he demands, taking illegal drugs in his van! His voice is raised. I look around, horrified. A customer looks up from her tomato sniffing to watch. My colleagues know my story, and seeing I was just traveling with this apparently insane man, who's to say it isn't true.

But it isn't. I've been clean as a whistle since we left. Max walks off this time as soon as Burt makes an appearance at the back of the store. Thank God they trust and support me through all of it.

Max still comes in on occasion, but more quietly, watching me from afar while he eyeballs the produce, until the day comes when he disappears from my world completely.

The dust settles. Days turn to weeks and to months. I find myself smiling in the magical fate of coming into this new place with this loving community and friends and the lush beauty and warmth of California. All of it is becoming my new life.

On my third month, I'm standing in front of the produce case in jean overalls, stacking a wall of romaine and red leaf lettuce, when I'm distracted by hysterical giggling by the entrance and look over.

Two boys in their mid twenties walk in. One of them meets my eyes.

He has a long face, a ring through his nose, and beautiful, wavy red hair that falls loose, down to his waist. Right away, he abandons his friend, swaggers towards me and stops abruptly before me with his hands innocently clasped in front. Bright blue eyes look to one side, then to the other, then to mine. He inhales excessively, as if he's about to give a speech.

"Um," he tips his head and narrows his eyes. "I've never seen you here in the organic section of our lovely Felton New Leaf. Hello, are you new here?"

A wide grin spreads over my face. This is a character.

"Laurel... and, a few months." I say.

"You're from around these parts I take it."

He giggles, lifts his arms, and wiggles his hips in place and then stops, clears his throat and stands exaggeratedly straight and offers me his hand

"Mr. Matthew Pink!"

"Laurel, where are you from; may I inquire?"

"Boston. I pause. But I'm not proud of it. Don't tell anyone."

He squaks, "Bawstan!' Pawk the Caw in Hawvaad Yaad!" pushes his chin down, and rolls exaggeratedly soft eyes up to me and blinks.

"Um, Laurel, can I have your phone number?"

I giggle and tip my head to the side.

"And what, pray tell, would you like my number for?"

He tips his head to the opposite side, mocking me.

"To play frisbee with me and my friend John of course, what else?"

With that, I write down my number on a piece of receipt, and he takes it and with the slip of paper in hand, goes running down the isle to meet back up with his friend and rounds the corner. A few minutes later, I look over to see his friend in line at the register. Matthew slides in behind him and looks over at me, grins and wiggles his fingers, then looks away with a serious face and bobs his head to the music playing on the overhead. They buy their groceries and on the way out the door, Matt waves the paper.

"Nice to meet you! I'll call you later!" He bows in Namaste, giggles and walks out.

I'm pleasantly surprised to discover Matthew meant what he'd said. He, John and I all went out to play frisbee, barefoot in an empty soccer field, and I managed to step on two honeybees that each stung me in the foot in one day. Frisbee would become a weekly ritual. John would go his own way and Matt would come over to sing, play guitar, and sometimes snuggle in my bed. I'm not attracted to him in the way he is with me. It can be a struggle, as I've never had such a fun-loving, trusted and creative friend. We tell each other everything. I'd like to be more attracted. And he's convinced we're something more regardless of my protest. Either way, I love his company and snuggling my face into his long red locks that smell of herb and Nag Champa.

It was perhaps a few months after meeting Matthew that my eyes began to follow a man named Raven who worked in what we call the dungeon; the cold, damp offices in the market's basement. Raven comes in on occasion to do marketing work for the store, so I rarely saw him, but after no more than two conversations, I became completely obsessed. I didn't want him to catch wind of my infatuation, but nevertheless found myself prattling on and on with my co-workers about my crush. He's mature and artistic, contemplative and eloquent. He writes beautiful poetry, and the dark eyes behind wire rim glasses speak only of depth, virtue and romance. He'd given me a CD he'd created, and every piece was breathtaking. That did it.

It was just a matter of time before he gained wind of my interest and comes up to invite me up the coast for dinner. My face turned crimson. Clearly I'm a pathetic, love, sick puppy dog. I could barely breathe as he was talking with me, but I nevertheless mustered a shy acceptance. As he walked away, I exhaled. He's way out of my league. I can sure talk it up with my friends at the store, but the idea of actually spending time alone with this man is terrifying.

He picks me up and we drive north along the ocean shore, up Rt. One. The sun sinks into the horizon. Grey clouds glow a soft underbelly of hazy orange, to pink, only to fade back to grey before blending into darkening skies.

I sit across from Raven at a restaurant on a deck over the water, shifting in my seat, my eyes darting as we wait for the waiter. Raven's perfectly comfortable. He smiles and tips the wine menu towards me, pointing out a Malbec, would I be interested in this one?

Thank God.

I take the menu and scan the list as if I might actually know enough about wine to choose something different.

"Yes," I say, "The Malbec looks the best."

When the waiter arrives, he pours samples for each of us. Raven's looking to me for approval, so I roll the wine around in the glass like I've watched others do and slowly take a sip, but I'm so nervous I can't swallow, so I sit there swishing wine in my mouth. Raven looks away to say a word to the waiter and I finally get it down.

"Oh, it's delicious." I say.

Raven nods in approval to the waiter, who pours our glasses half full and wraps a white napkin around the neck of the bottle before leaving it on the table.

I have to admit, the wine really is quite delicious. While I'm cautious to drink, I nevertheless really want to lighten up and enjoy this time with Raven.

And the wine does help. A lot.

We eat. He pays. And I manage a half intelligent conversation without too much blundering while he drives me home.

I realize I've never actually been on real date before.

Once we finally reach my driveway, he parks and my hand is already pulling the handle open when the ignition goes off, and I begin to step out.

"Laurel." Raven's voice beckons from behind.

I look back at him and he caresses my chin. I close the door enough so the overhead light goes back out, and he slowly pulls into me for a long, delicious kiss.

Raven and I spend foggy evenings walking on the Santa Cruz boardwalk, and share the deepest parts of our selves. He's recently divorced, only a year ago, from a fifteen-year marriage. He has a house he'd made with her and wants to finish renovating it and get it on the market. He's in transition. In fact, he'll be leaving the store soon, perhaps in the next few months to find another job and a place to settle in.

I ask if he's still in love with his wife. He says yes.

I wish I hadn't asked.

Things change with love and his words, 'settle in', stick strong in my mind. Perhaps he and I might settle in together in time.

I don't mention my past with alcohol and drugs quite the same way as I had to Burt and Ernie at the store. Only that things in childhood were rough, and I hope to one day channel some of the pain and passions into art. I think that would be so rich and healing. What medium? Oh, I don't know. I suppose I've had fantasies of working with clay. I think I'd be good at it. But I've never actually taken the initiative to begin. Really, I've only just begun to settle in. But maybe I'll take a class one day.

We make a weekly ritual of eating fine meals and getting loose lipped on red wine before he brings me home to make love, and he touches me like no other man has, precisely the way I've always wanted to be loved. I caress his face and his neck, every part of him, in the deepest adoration I've ever felt for a man, even for Ben.

He meets my eyes, making love to me slow and intimate, loving and caring for me completely; my world became Raven.

On a Friday night as I arrive home from work, there on the deck next to Jack, bearing his teeth in a doggie grin, whining and tail wagging wildly, is a block of porcelain white clay. On top of the clay is one of his CD's, and a perfect red rose. Nothing could have delighted me more.

Well, except for Matthew who's arrived to hang out and play guitar. He looks at me, smiles and places his guitar against the house without a word, and sits on the deck chair across from me to roll a joint. I've begun smoking with him on occasion, promising myself not to go to far into it. Both of us thoroughly stoned, Matthew picks up the guitar and sings 'Another Lonely Day' by Ben Harper.

Later that evening, Matthew and I take a last puff of the joint before he takes off to meet up with John. Excited, I take the clay into my room, pop Raven's music into my player, set down some newspaper, and sink myself in. I remember some of the basics I once read in a sculpting book: I have to knead out air bubbles and keep it damp. I don't have any tools or idea how I'd fire a finished piece, but I'm so excited to sink my fingers in, I have to start.

I play around with the conception of a few ideas, but something more interesting arises: a face, an expression in the clay developing, so I try following it's direction, allowing my ideas to fall away.

My fingers trace lines: a nose, eyes and mouth come alive. It's a woman: an intense woman at that. Her neck arches, the apex of her brow sharp, and her mouth opens into a grimace and her tongue lolls in rapture. Thick ribbons of hair flow down, meeting soft, thrashing shoulders down to the smooth line of her bust. The dark, mischievous tone of Raven's music moves my fingers further into her expression, and I become lost in the mirror of my perception come alive, what awaits to be revealed from deep inside.

An image of my mother's face arises. I'm six years old, sitting on the floor in my living room when I look up to see her there, arms folded, leaning her shoulder into the archway. Her dark lashes damp and clustered, half moon circles underline dark eyes, tensions crease between low brows, and deep lines follow the corners of her frown. She glares at me, looking through me, as if I'm not even there. I hold my breath, waiting.

My mind jumps forward.

I'm seventeen, in the bathroom of the convenience store where I work, ripping open a second box of menstrual pads. Blood came gushing out when I was behind the counter, and I ran back to the toilet and the blood just kept coming. I was the only one watching the store, so I put in a tampon and a thick pad, rinse my hands and ran back to the counter to ring the line up fast. I still felt blood pouring out, and rushed back to the toilet. I ran back and forth like this every few minutes, going through a box each of pads and tampons, drenching them all in forty minutes. I figured I was having a miscarriage. I wasn't careful enough. I called my mother. I hadn't spoken with her since I ran.

When she answers I tell her I'm loosing blood fast. I think I need to go to the hospital. It's not a good time to call, she tells me. She's busy at work right now.

I didn't say anything else. I couldn't explain further.

I just went numb and hung up the phone. I didn't need the hospital. The blood stopped soon after that anyway.

The song on Raven's CD switches and I glance over to my bedside table, at the snapshot of my high school graduation.

My grandmother. My mother. And myself: my face bloated from alcohol.

"Goodnight." Greg says, popping his face in the door.

Startled, I look up from the clay.

"Oh, goodnight Greg, sleep well. Oh, I'm sorry, I'll turn the music off now." I pull together a smile.

"Keep it on if you like, I like it, actually. I'm glad you're here, Laurel. You sleep well too." He taps the wall and disappears.

I think hours may have passed, but I've been so absorbed I haven't noticed Greg or the exhaustion settled in. I lean back to take a better look at her.

Intense.

It will take two weeks to complete her. Even longer to recognize her face from a book I'd come upon on the Hindu pantheon of Gods and Goddesses, She is Kali:

"The Black One."

"The Bringer of Death."

Raven and I enjoy months of candle lit nights together. I fall more deeply in love, while he becomes ever more occupied with house renovations, preparing for a new life and a new job. I try to be patient and understanding while he calls less and less. He stops showing up at the market.

And then he doesn't call at all.

I've always known; it was never the same for him. He's respectable. He has it together, his own house and his own life and a career. I'm just a junkie and a whore.

He doesn't want me, and I can't live without him.

So when I'm home, I sit by the phone wishing he'd call, but he doesn't.

I call him, again, against my better judgment. He's cordial, but I can hear it. He's gone. My hand shakes as I hang up the phone.

•

I'm sitting at a table, rolling a cigarette on the back deck of the coffee house, on my break, across the street from the market. Distracted, I gaze up to find a boy with black hair down to his waist, scrambling over the wall that separates us from Mr. Chung's Noodle House.

He looks to me with his hands on his hips, checking out the empty tables surrounding us, then climbs over the back of the chair across from me and sinks in with a sigh, unpacks papers and tobacco from his bag, and busies himself with his roll.

I stare.

"Um," A wide grin sweeps across his face. "Mind if I smoke?"

I look back down at my roll.

I mutter, "Do I have a choice?"

He thrusts a hand out to me.

"Aloha. Kopono."

"Hi," I take his hand, "Laurel," and pull it back to lick my paper.

"Hold on, hold on," he places a hand over my roll "Let me add something nice to that."

He shuffles through his bag, bringing out a tiny glass jar, and unscrews the cap.

"Try this." I pull back. He's clearly an island boy. "I don't want to get stoned. Thanks."

"Stoned! No, no, no. Don't worry." He looks around. "Who said anything about getting stoned? This is herbal. Yummy. Better for you too." He pushes.

I'm skeptical, and take the jar and lift it to my nose to smell: mullein, sage, lavender, mugwort... no pot.

"OK. Fine. Just a little." I let him sprinkle a pinch over my tobacco, tuck it all in, and twist. I lift my lighter, but he interrupts with a flame before me. I shoot him a look, inhale slow, and sigh heavy smoke out.

"Hmmn." I look at the cigarette between my fingers. *Here I am smoking again.*

"It is nice." I say "Thanks."

It won't take much. Right now, I'm open season.

Kopono's the polar opposite of Raven. He jumps around light and free, stirring things up, walking a fine line between adverse and inspiring. I'm always a little uneasy around him, but the distraction's welcome from my heartache for Raven.

We pass a joint back and forth on my porch on a hot afternoon after work. I watch him as he's speaking, barely hearing his words, fascinated with the picture before me. Never have I seen a more Christ-like image upon a man's face. My body shutters and I melt into the ecstasy of him. Yet just as soon as I sink into affections for him, he looks upward into the sky, and he's suddenly transformed into the likes of Satan, the fallen angel. I don't believe in the Devil, never mind know what he looks like, but beyond logic, he's here in front of me; my stomach contracts.

He looks back down. Only Kopono.

Kopono and I become lovers, and sex with him is like eating a candy bar: filling space without any nutrition. On an afternoon that Matthew's over playing guitar with us, I'm about to leave the bathroom when Kopono steps in. He wants to make love there and then. I look away, telling him I don't want to; Matt's here.

"Matt is a blade of grass," he insists.

"Matt's my friend. Come on."

He pushes. I push against him. He pushes again. I give in. We fuck, leaning against the bathroom sink. As soon as we're done I yank my clothes on and run out to find Matt. He's already gone.

A few weeks into it, Kopono suggests we take ecstasy. I agree. It's a good idea. Perhaps my heart will open to him. But that night, even high, I'm insecure around him. He wants to make love. It's a week past my moon, so I request we use a condom, but he protests. He hates them. OK. I won't demand it, but please, I tell him, please be careful.

Before I know it, Kopono's moaning and thrusting hard into me. *My God, is he coming?* I push his hips in a panic, trying to get him out. "Kopono! What are you doing?" He makes no attempt to leave, but instead, plants his seed deep. I protest, pleading with him as to why he'd do such a thing. But it was too late. It was done.

Several weeks later, I'm at work early in the morning and run to the toilet to vomit. I take a test that confirms and call Kopono. My worst nightmare has come true.

He responds like a cool breeze; what am I worried about? It'll be no problem for me to keep the baby. It's natural. Women do it all the time.

I can grow a few plants, and I'd have all I need. He's going back to Hawaii in a few months. Maybe I could find a way to live there too. I didn't expect this nonchalant response. I don't know what to say.

I tell him I'll talk to him later and hang up the phone.

Grow a few plants? I've never grown herb before. I have a roommate, who's sober. Is he serious? I'm in California. That would be illegal. How?

I'm doing my best to sit with what he's saying...could it really be that easy? I'm considering if there's any spark of hope in a situation like this. He's not going to remain as a father, nor was he offering any support. That was clear.

"Women do it all the time."

He makes it sound so easy... but, with no home or family? I've never had money. I'm not capable of lovingly raising a child. But I would never pass on what I experienced as a child. Surely I'd fall in love...wouldn't I?

But the last twelve years on drugs, and conceived on drugs too. What are the chances it would be healthy?

I called in sick to work and pace and scream and sit and cry- my mind racing for days- back and forth, yes and no. What *is* right? Nothing's clear. I hold my stomach and rock.

I have to be realistic. I don't have money to take care of myself, never mind a baby. But how can I possibly abort? But with no support, it's impossible: How can I bring a child into this world? I can't justify either decision. How did I let this happen?

No one called. Not Raven. Not Kopono. I'm trapped alone on a runaway train.

After a week of debating with myself passes, exhausted, I call Matthew. I tell him what's going on. Yes, he says, eyes glassy with tears, he'll take me.

I call Kopono as well, informing him I've made a decision, and I need his help. It's six hundred dollars. I'd like him to pay half?

Kopono roars over the other line: "You have no respect asking for that!"

My stomach is a rock. I hang up the phone, and scream at the top of my lungs.

My last call is Raven. He's the only person I know who's economically stable. I'm horrified to ask, but I don't have time, and I'm in trouble.

Raven comes over. We talk and he leaves three hundred dollars in my room. If the day comes when you can return the money that's fine, but don't worry over it. Just take care of yourself, he says. That's the last time I see Raven.

I wake up in a cold, sterile room in the hospital. At twenty-seven, I'm living my worst nightmare, my image of hell. It's also my turning point, when I can no longer deny how far I've been from myself: the true beginning steps of healing.

Chapter 10 ~ Meeting Father Ron

I 'd since moved into a farmhouse in the quiet hills of California, in an attempt- once again- to start over.

I put my head down and worked, remaining quiet and alone for another year at the store. And as the winter months came to pass, I felt the stirrings of a new chapter of life soon to begin. Almost over night, an irrational, unjustified knowing fell upon me: I'd soon be doing something creative for a living.

I was so convinced in some naive, childlike way, that I gave Burt thirty days, and went around the store telling everyone, "Soon, I'll be doing something creative for a living." Perhaps it made the idea more concrete and real, but I had not the slightest clue, nor details.

I didn't know myself what I was talking about...and yet some part of me was completely clear of what was next.

On my last week I was training my replacement. I have enough money for a month's rent, and no plan. I began to wonder about myself. Why have I gone around playing childish games? Am I incapable of getting a grip on reality, too damaged and insane? I'm in my room in bed writing these thoughts in my journal, when a new roommate climbs the steps to my room to introduce him self. He pops his head in and gives a gentle knock. I look up.

"Hello?" He's a thin, blonde man in his early forties with doe blue eyes, wearing a short rim hat, with a feather tucked in the side.

"Hello, I'm Johnny. May I come in a moment?"

He waves a finger towards the room across the way.

"I believe I'll be living down the hall from you."

I tap my bed, inviting him to sit.

He tells me he's just come back from Burning Man, and it was profound. Just amazing! I tell him I've never heard of it. Is it a festival?

"Oh, you've never gone? Wow. This is my fifth year in a row!"

He's the lead musician for an improvisational performance group that will soon be going out on its first summer tour. He's on his way to bed, he'll tell me more in the morning, breakfast? Johnny leaves and I undress and slide under the covers.

Festivals and a traveling performance group; wouldn't life be amazing like that.

"It's called The Living Oracle," Johnny tells me, tearing a bite size piece of toast, buttering it, and mopping up soft egg yolk on his plate.

"We perform live improvisational Tarot readings for the audience: there's six or seven performers, all channeling three or four each of the twenty two Major Arcana of the Tarot."

He's lost me. 'Major Arcana?' 'Channel?'

"We're using archetypes to help people heal."

I still don't understand, but I'm really curious.

"Try-outs are in two weeks in Texas. Your look is perfect, you know. Why don't you come see if you could make it with the group?"

Holy shit, is he serious...me?

I'm terribly excited about the idea, but this is way over my head. I have no idea about the Tarot or what an archetype is, let alone channel one. The last time I was in front of an audience was in high school theatre: I walk out on stage, look out at everyone staring at me, and went completely blank. I couldn't even muster 'I forgot my lines,' I just stood there, frozen like a deer in the headlights. But even more disconcerting than all of that, Johnny informed me that if I don't make the group, apparently I'm on my own. That means I'd be stuck in a city I've never been to and don't know anybody, with no money, in Texas. I imagine Budweiser, barbecue ribs and red, white and blue flags. Thoughts spin through my head until I look up to find Johnny, chewing and smirking at me, clearly entertained.

"Well?" he pushes.

I shake my head in bewilderment.

"How much time do I have?"

I'm laying in bed, in a small trailer at the end of a driveway in San Antonio, Marco's place, Johnny's friend. We've begun tryouts. There's a group of nine of us, every one of them is outrageously beautiful and talented. Three won't make it; I'm doomed.

Cathryn, the producer, has given us pages to study up on the archetypes. I pour over them, but it's so much information, not a heck of a lot is sinking in. Exhausted, I place my studying aside and turn off the light, wondering how I'll manage.

I'm the only one that's not already part of the community, and I don't get the impression that Cathryn likes me all that much. In our meeting today, she gave us an assignment: act out the innermost pain within you. On my turn, I went right into it without any forethought.

I threw myself down in the lap of the oldest man in the group, grabbed his shirt, pulling myself into him and him to me, search into his eyes, and plead: "Please...love me! Love me!" Repeating this intensely, over and over again. When I completed, the silence was haunting.

Oh my god, what did I just do? The faces around me were all somewhere between awe and horror of my display- that was all too real.

Images of the day come and fade, trailing into sleep, then startling awake from the howl of winds that pick up quickly.

Leaves whip in circles outside the screen door, and chimes on the deck of the house next door, bang out of rhythm. Wind whistles through moonlit branches that send shadows dancing through the trailer. The sound of a scream flies through winds above. The poison of fear trickles into my blood as cool air slides across my skin. Another blood curdling scream from above, of a woman being tortured. Fright courses through my veins and my breath runs quick and short. The screen door flies open and swings, squealing from its hinges. Metal and bamboo chimes all clang chaotically. From behind and above me, a woman screams three times, as if floating there in mid air, North, then West, then East. Horror engulfs me. My heart pounds in my chest. All that I am is fear, growing ever more intense.

WHAM! The door flies shut and I choke and gasp awake, in a bed in a trailer, in the silent, still Texas night.

That morning I wake up weary, drag myself out of bed and throw on a long collared shirt Johnny left hanging on a hook by the door, and make my way to the house, finding him and Marco chatting over coffee at the table.

I pour myself a cup and slide in, next to Johnny.

"You guys sleep ok last night?" Marco asks.

Piercing blue eyes look through me. Perhaps he's noticing circles under my eyes. I barely slept a wink.

"I forgot to warn you two about our friendly neighborhood screech owl. She was busy around these parts last night."

"*That* was an owl?"

My dreams come flooding back into memory.

"I, God I had some crazy dreams from that thing."

"Yeah." Marco giggles. "You know once I had a friend from New York stay in there 'bout this time last year. He's this big black muscle head," Marcos nods, giggling like a kid, "And you know, he comes a-runnin' in here in the dead of the night, shaking like a leaf, crying 'Marco! Marco! Some crazy bitch is screamin' out there like she in hell! New York ain't got nothin' scary on this Texas shit!"

We're all cracking up and Johnny shuffles through his bag.

"Hey Laurel, Cathryn stopped by late last night and dropped these off for you."

He places three Tarot cards on the table, sliding them towards me.

"She said look them over for today. She thinks these are your archetypes."

I pull them towards me, eyes wide.

"No way!" I say, "I didn't think I was going to make it!"

I look up at Johnny. "She likes me?"

"Well," Johnny looks at me sideways, "you didn't make it yet, but ya, it looks good."

I look through the cards: The High Priestess, the Universe, and the Moon. I stop and stare at the Moon card. She's a woman in a purple robe, with a full moon behind her. An owl is perched on her shoulder, and her face looks in three different directions: North, West, and East.

Johnny and I drive through country roads between fields of tall, flowing grass that wave in the Texas winds. We pull into a gravel driveway in front of a brown, shingled farmhouse, windows lit with candlelight. We're walking to the door that opens to Jenna- a young, gentle blonde woman with smiling, fairy blue eyes. I'd met her a week before at tryouts with her husband Christian, admiring the both of them. She hugs me warmly, and looks into my eyes. "Goddess," she says.

She's calling *me* Goddess?

I direct her attention to Johnny, and hear my name. Several of the others in the Oracle are languidly snuggled on a massive pile of pillows, inviting me to join.

I've never snuggled with anyone but my boyfriends, in private. I'm a mouse looking for the right spot in a pile of snakes.

Jenna catches my attention and kneels down, offering me a wine glass, full with a murky, brown liquid.

"It's mushroom tea." She hands it to me with her twinkling fairy eyes and an impish smile.

I return her affections and settle onto an elbow. She takes the pillow next to me and calls over to a man a named Jeshua who's speaking to a curly red headed woman with overflowing cleavage close by. A beautiful man, maybe fifty-five with shining green eyes, comes over and kisses Jenna on the cheek.

"This is my husband Jeshua," she says.

'Wait- I thought...'

She shoots me a mischievous grin.

"I have two Divine husbands," she says, "Christian *and* Jeshua!" She lifts her foot to disclose a second wedding band on her toe.

"Oh," I say, looking into Jeshua's green eyes. He's older, more like a father, and Christian's a thirty something artist and musician. She prattles on about 'conscious relationship,' and I'm curious if I'm closed, full of judgment, but I see this as more of a practical picture than purely from love, as she's portraying. She walks away in her flowing robes to attend to others. I'm intrigued and full of questions.

Having drunken all of my tea, my belly rolls, telling me I'll soon be on a journey. It's no time for inquiries now. I thank Jeshua, and rise on wobbly legs to search out a good place to settle.

I follow a long hall to a side door and automatically open it, catching sight of naked bodies, and almost slam it tight, but before I could, I hear my name called out from inside. Timidly pushing the door open again, I scan the room. There's maybe twenty people, some I've befriended, including Johnny. Some are lazing on the bed, sharing fruit and giggling, others move about, serving water or wine, teasing and joking.

The perfect place beckons me on the edge of an enormous bed, so I slip in, remove my clothes to fit in with the rest, making myself a nest with them, and perch myself there to take it all in.

Friends take turns telling stories, shape shifting into their characters. A beautiful woman with sharp blue eyes and waist long blond hair kneels next to me and tells me of her totem animal. The pale skin of her hands and face turn black, and a panther stretches out on the bed before me. Infinite faces pass, monstrous and divine, from one to the next.

"What more would thee have from Goddess graces?" asks the red haired woman I'd seen speaking with Jeshua, in response to her friend at the other side of the room.

"Thy golden breast and sultry lips pleases thee indeed, Madam, and is surely enough to send thy soul into eternal rapture. Yet if thy must be sentenced to the bonds of prudence, I shall most graciously settle for thine ambrosial wine!" A bottle is passed across the bed, and I realize that I've been in a room where everyone is naked, and not once have I felt dirty or leered at.

Suddenly in my peripheral is a luminous blue. I turn and am met by a stunning blond man with eyes like the sky. He knees down before me, and looks into me as if in worship, surrounded by an electric aura of blue.

"Goddess," he says.

I've never seen him with these eyes, but I know this man. He leans up and kisses me with soft breath on my forehead, and returns to our gaze. I meet his tenderness, watching him watching me. He kisses my left breast, then the other, and returns to trace my cheek with his hand. The thought crosses my mind that such abrupt behavior would send me reeling in any other circumstance, but I trust this man completely. I fall in love with him then and there, smiling with him as if we'd seen each other through a million lifetimes already.

"Hello," I say, delighted, and run my fingers through his beautiful blond locks.

Johnny's voice cuts in from behind, proclaiming that these kinds of behaviors are too much for me. How dare he! I look at Stephen and smile at the absurdity of the tone coming from behind. My suitor was calm, and in perfect understanding in the moment of the game, rises, apologizes to Johnny, and excuses himself. I remain quiet as a sleeping kitten.

I didn't see that man again until the early morning hours just before I was leaving to go home to the trailer, when we found a last moment together. He pulls me aside into an empty room and we kiss passionately in parting. His name is Stephen, and he'd like to see me again.

I'm looking at the freckle-covered nose of a young girl, maybe 12. She pulls three cards, the first is flipped over: The Moon. I don't know if I heard any of her inquiry, but I see myself in her eyes. She's seen so much already.

I stand up and walk towards her, looking into her dark eyes, then to the skies, and cry out:

"WHY CAN'T I JUST BE A LITTLE GIRL!"

Other words come that I don't recall and when I come back to my senses and look into the crowd, the girl has her face in her hands, and most of the audience is in tears or stunned. There's nothing else to do or say, so I sit back down and the crowd is still until the next card jumps up and shifts the mood.

It was a powerful moment, as many have been. All summer, each costume and mask has given me the freedom to speak into what I see and know, permission to transform into someone wise and powerful. Never before have I been so seen. Suddenly I'm in the limelight. Suddenly I'm worshipped and respected.

Frankly, against all I'd expected, the attention's overwhelming. I escape at the completion of the shows, running from the kind of recognition I'd thought I wanted.

But this time we were packing right away, so I stuck around, and a man approached to introduce him self. He's tall and dark, perhaps with Native American blood. Beautiful honey locks fall over muscular, tan shoulders. He's been on the same festival route as our bus. He's been to every show and loves our performances. His name is Ron, and he'd like to take a stroll together before tonight's shows. I'd been avoiding the groupies, but yes, there's something about him. We walk together towards my tent and Ron strides head first, watching with inquisitive blue eyes as he inquires into the summer's journey. His grin is childlike and mischievous, reaching from ear to ear and as we walk.

He points out an RV we're passing on the way, stopping to tell me it's his.

"Would you like to come in and take a shower?" I've come to learn, the chance to have a real shower is a precious thing on a festival route.

Warm water pours over my face and Ron asks me from the other room.

"So, what's your full name?"

"Laurel Yonika."

Ron shows up and is standing there naked in front of me with a towel wrapped around his head.

"Did you say your last name is, Yoni-ka?"

"Yes." I say, giggling.

His eyes go sideways. "How do you spell that?"

"Y-O-N-I-K-A" I say, rinsing shampoo from my hair.

"Oh," he says, raising his brows. "Now *that* is a *really* interesting name."

He turns and walks out of sight. A moment later I hear him from the bedroom:

"Um, would you like I wash your back?" He shows up again in the doorframe, this time with a washcloth in his hand. *What the heck, he's safe.*

"Okay." I say. "Just washing," and he squeezes in behind me and runs the warm, soapy washcloth over my back, rinses me, then goes to work scrubbing himself. When we were complete, he wraps a towel snug round my body, like a father would wrap his child, and invites me to lay with him, to talk on his bed.

Ron lay down next to me, leaning himself up on a pillow and looks into my eyes, explaining to me that he's what is called a "Daka" or a "Tantric Sexual healer." He is known as "Father Ron." I have no idea what he's getting at, but I'm already crossing the line into discomfort and considering a polite escape. But I tell myself I should be open to this. After all, I do have a pretty messed up sexual history, so if he's a healer, this is probably the best place for me to be.

He asks about my dad. This is weird- so fast- but he does seem genuinely concerned.

I tell him I don't have a dad. I was created by aliens.

He stares.

"Okay," I sigh. "I don't really know my dad. I met him for the first time since he left when I was a baby around..." my eyes roam to their top right corners, "I don't know, maybe nine or ten."

"My mom demanded he take some responsibility with my older brother and I. He lived an hour and a half away, and picked us up a few weekends that year to bring us back to his house. My brother was stealing and getting in trouble. She couldn't handle him, so she called my dad. And it was great- I loved it there. I had the ultimate step mom. Really, if I could have had it my way, I'd have lived there all the time. The only thing that was weird was being in the car with him. He'd do weird stuff like run his hand over my leg and say "incest is best," and things like that. I mean...I know he was joking, but it still felt weird. On one of those weekends I was over, his neighbor Mary once told me that she'd seen him cry before, and it was when he was talking about me and my brother, so I knew that he cared."

Father Ron wraps his arms around me and lets me snuggle into his chest. I love that feeling. I love it more than anything, just to feel safe and loved in a man's strong, safe arms.

Chapter 11 ~ A Brother's Love

I pull into a barren parking lot with sparse patches of grass growing through cracks in cement. There's a dumpster on the far side corner, with a plastic bag overflowing with empty beer cans. Grabbing my bag, I step out of the car and shove the door closed with the sole of my boot. I catch glimpses of cars on the highway behind the condos, passing fast through a wall of conical pines, as I climb a short set of plain cement stairs, up to the front door. I enter into a dark hall, pungent with old cooking and cigarettes. Stairs lead up and down to various floors, and I climb up to the first door on the right, number 9.

"Hi there, little sis!"

Long, chestnut curls fall over his shoulders. He's grinning ear to ear, and he opens his long, tattoo-covered arms wide.

"Big brother!"

I jump into his hug. It's been twelve years since we've seen each other.

"Come in, come in," he says.

I step in, watching him. He's always been handsome, but I'd never seen him look very healthy. His puppy brown eyes are as soft as they've ever been; regardless of the life he's lived, with long, dark lashes, and telltale dark circles underneath.

The apartment is completely white-walled with no art, but there are puppets and muppets and marionettes, hanging all around the living room on random hooks and nails. Ghoulish monster toys stand poised on top of a massive television set, and Kermit the frog and Animal hang from the corners. Star-Wars action figures still in their boxes sit atop his computer. A Chucky doll in a rainbow shirt with a nasty grin on its face and wild, orange hair sits in the corner. Stacks of books and baseball card collections cover the coffee table, and the corners of Playboy magazines jut from the cubbies beneath.

I sigh.

"Come look at this, little sis!"

He's got his hand on the knob to the door next to the kitchen and opens it, grandly gesturing.

"This is your room! You stay here as long as you want, little sis."

I put down my bags down and sit on the bed and bounce to give it a feel.

"It's really good to see you, big brother."

Living with my brother will take some adjustment. He lives on beer, candy bars and TV dinners, and is perpetually glued to his seat in front of a video game. He plays with people from all around the world, he informs me. They have relationships, meetings, bartering systems, an entire virtual community, he says. He's spent so much time on his character, he's worth thousands, and like so many of the things he's collecting, he'll one day be able to sell that character for good money.

He's been on the road to fulfilling his dreams. Several months ago, he'd passed a test for employment through Verizon, and is on a mission to climb the corporate ladder so he can one day have a wife and a family.

I'd brought Matt some clay pieces I had made, and pull them out for him. There's a wizard, with a long white beard and a concentrated expression on his face. He holds a marble crystal ball in one hand while the other hovers over it, casting spells. I brought a dragon, and a frog with a crown on his head and pursed lips ready to kiss...and a bald man, hatching naked from an egg, gazing skyward in awe and wonder. Matt loved my artistic side, and I guess it motivated him, because on the following Friday after work, he brings home bright acrylic paints and stands there, waving his finger at the white walls and demands I paint. I reason that our uncle, the landlord, will have our heads, but he just holds his ground and points, "Paint, woman!"

Matt sits down one night and presses pause on his video game- that tells me he's serious- and says he wants to know...

"What happened with Dad?"

"I might need a smoke for this," I say, and fall into the couch, gathering my pouch of tobacco. He watches me roll.

"Well, I guess it was about two months ago now when I called him. I had the idea that if we spent some time together after all these years, maybe I could work through some of the stuff you and I went through. Maybe it was a dumb idea. I don't know, Matt, I've just been a mess."

"I was coming from California and headed cross-country with my boyfriend Phillip when I called him. I told him I wanted to get to know him; maybe it would help me get life straightened out. He told me he'd have to talk to Carolyn and had me call back the next day, and I guess they decided that they had work around the house, so I could come and help."

"I was psyched. I really felt like I needed to be with him, and Carolyn too. I don't know what your take on her was, but to me, she was like the ultimate, mega- mom."

I walk over to sit by the door, so the smoke will go out, into the hall.

"Anyway, I get there and they both put me to work. Dad had garden projects and Carolyn had me painting her batiks, you remember those?" Matt nods.

"I was happy to help with it, actually, I looked at it like a kind of apprenticeship; it would only help me learn more. Anyway, I worked my ass off for a month and a half for all the work they handed me before I had any free time, which was fine. I liked the work. But I have to admit, it felt a little weird sometimes, with Jen, Michael, and Chris always coming and going to all their sports and projects and stuff. It kind of made me a little jealous- I guess I've always been. I'm thinking, like, aren't I my father's daughter too? I can only imagine where I'd be if I had the advantages they had. But whatever, it was fine. I was happy to be there and have the opportunity, so mostly I was ok with it."

"But then one day I'm in the garden, mixing bags of soil and amendment into a wheel barrel. Dad walks up to me like he usually did with his arms held wide and we hug. But then it was weird, he grabs a handful of the mix, and suddenly his hand is up my shirt rubbing dirt over my belly. We're laughing and I'm going down to the ground, but now his hands are rubbing over my breasts. At that point I don't know why, but I just kind of sit there in a stupor."

"He pulls his hand out and leans back up and looks at me, still chuckling, and I muster a smile too, but I fake it, I just don't know how to respond. I watch him walk away, patting the dirt from his hands on his pants, and I start working again. I decide I am being paranoid."

"But around that same time, things were starting to feel weird with Carolyn, too. One of the kids told me she said I was 'nickel and diming' her, which was a shock because I was working so hard, and I was buying my own groceries. So then I started walking on ice a bit, feeling awkward, wondering if I was stepping over the line to have a cup of coffee in the morning- you know?"

I pause and inhale smoke deep and blow it into the hall.

"She'd given me some clay from the kid's projects she'd stored downstairs, and when her batiks were finished, I'd started making pieces, and filled the kiln a few times. One of my pieces was pretty sexual; it was a replica of a carving from an old Indian temple, two women and a man. I liked the piece a lot. Dad *definitely* liked it. But I think it was after she saw that piece that the tension in the air got really thick."

"What was happening was not completely clear, but nothing was directly said. At the same time, I was getting nervous. My money was running down to my last hundred dollars and there was a labyrinth of questions between that point and my next paycheck. With the end so near, I was becoming less keen to share the groceries I was getting with my siblings, and asked them to cool it and stick to what their parents were buying them. It was a hard thing to say, but it was three to one and, fuck, you know, I just didn't know what was next, I needed to stretch it."

"But I think that was the last straw. Carolyn avoided me, and one of my sisters ceased speaking at all to me after I made that request. I realized then, I hadn't communicated where my concerns were coming from, and anyway, how could any of them possibly- in their experience- understand? I felt like shit. I'd set a terrible example. I was guilty and angry with myself for showing up without having more, anything really, to give to any of them. But apologizing was to no avail. Carolyn and my sister apparently decided I was whoever they decided I was."

"But then, believe it or not, things got worse. My father and I were sitting, talking at the top of the staircase. Seemingly from nowhere, he made a very casual and peculiar proposition; 'Why don't we sleep together?' I sighed and considered a moment, maybe I was being paranoid again. Perhaps he just meant, do I want to take a *nap* with him. So I told him, 'No, I'm not sleepy,' but then he asks 'Why, are you uncomfortable with your body?' I just looked at him a moment, waiting, as if he might say the punch line. But nothing comes. I looked down and took a pause to be clear with myself what was happening, wondering if this could still be a misinterpretation. I stared at the ceramic frog I'd made for him with the contemplative face, and told him I don't want that because I am his daughter. Nothing else was said. I just sat there next to him, silent, wondering what to do. I figured, no real harm done, it was just a question, and I got up, and told him I was going for a walk, and went down the stairs... and that was it."

"But truth is, I think I shut down then. I couldn't figure out what was going on in my own head, never mind everyone else's enough to reasonably open a conversation. I was upset, but really, it was just a damn question. I wasn't hurt, and I wanted things to work out so much. But I severely fucked up with the groceries thing with Carolyn and the kids, and I took a few more days to try to clear my head, but Carolyn and my sister weren't letting up, and the tension of the silence was unbearable. So I gathered my things and got the hell out of there."

"That's when I called mom, and I don't know, I was just freaking out. Like, I'd somehow hit my last wall. Amazing really, after all I've toughed it out through, it's a question that knocks me flat on my ass."

I chuckle and shake my head, staring off into the ribbons of smoke moving through the hall.

"So Mom suggested I come here, so here I..."

I look over at my brother. His face is deep crimson red. He looks like he's going to blow.

I backpedal.

"But, I'm totally alright now, I mean, I just got sad, but now I'm fine, I'm not even mad."

"I mean, the rest of my time there was fine, I just..."

Matt seethes.

"That fucking man is scum."

I wake late on a cold, snowy morning, relieved I don't have to trudge through the snow that's piling outside in order to catch a train and get to class, its Saturday. A few more months of this, and I'm finally done, I'll have my degree.

I crawl out of bed and walk past Matt, already on his video game. He waves an enormous Dunkin Donuts, orange and brown lettered Styrofoam cup in the air.

"Mornin' little sis!"

"Mmmnn," I return, and do a double, take. His cup looks more like a bucket.

I plop myself on the couch and fish for the tobacco hidden in the drawer of the coffee table, blinking at Matt's video screen. His character jumps and thrashes, making sounds that have become a permanent part of my background. I roll my cigarette, set it aside for later, stretch, and lumber to the kitchen. Looking back at him from behind the counter, there's something amusing about the character that he is, playing another character with such focused determination. Tattoos cover every bit of his legs and arms not covered by a short, blue terry-cloth robe.

I open the fridge: rice milk and broccoli. Broccoli's the only green thing I've managed to get him to eat, and then only when doused in cheese.

I grab the rice milk and berries from the freezer, and pour milk into the blender. Banana, berries, and tap in the last of the spirulina. Last night's dream flashes through my thoughts, but I don't fully catch it.

I look over to my brother.

"Hey Matt, did you have recurring dreams when you were a kid?'"

"Um-hmm." He shifts in his seat, pauses his game, and looks thoughtfully out the window, sipping from his cup.

He looks over.

"Yeah, and I had it again, maybe a year or two ago. It's really quick: two cannons are facing each other, and they go off at the same time, right into each other. It's this crazy explosion," His hands wave around, "and from there it's this massive war in my head. That's it, then I wake up. I had it all the time when I was a kid."

'Huh.' I murmur.

The dream is so simple, it stumps me; seems a bit much for the proverbial inner struggle.

"In school," I tell him, "I'm taking a class on dream interpretation. My teacher says that the key is to think of the characters and situations as aspects of your self, your own symbolic information system. So, if you dream of a friend, it doesn't necessarily mean you're receiving a message about that friend, but rather it's an invitation to understand your symbolic perception of that friend and how they might represent a part of yourself."

I pause.

"But your dream is, hmmn."

My eyes roll up and right and I tap my finger on my chin, meet his gaze, and shake my head as if satisfied. "Clearly you're just way messed up."

Matt sneers, growls and leaps out of his seat, bolting after me into the kitchen. I squeal, grab the jar of spirulina, and shake it in front of him. "Spirulina!" I yell, holding it like a cross to a vampire.

Matt stops fast in his tracks and gasps. He grabs at his throat, sticks his tongue out and makes wheezing noises. I step forward, shaking the bottle and he falls, sprawling to the floor, twitches and jumps several times, and expires.

Satisfied, I walk away. Matt lifts his head.

"Is it gone?"

"It's gone."

I blend my drink and pour a thick green glass when my brother's head pops up and the corners of his mouth go down as he crinkles his forehead. He holds his hand out and I help him up to go back to his game while I sit on the couch and mock him with lip-smacking noises.

"Pond-scum," he says, scrunching his nose and shaking his head. Admittedly, this morning's consistency seems a bit off, some bits in the mix, *probably from the berries*, but take several gulps anyway. I catch a piece in my teeth and spit it out to investigate. I wipe the liquid away and find a little tear of paper adherent to my finger. Suspect, I wipe again, and find the words: 'not eat.'

"Uh-oh."

I must have blended the spirulina-drying packet into my smoothie, and I had already drunk over half of it.

"Um, Matt, we may have a little problem. I think I just poisoned myself."

I tell him what's happened and he calmly pauses his game, gets up, slides on a jacket and tells me we're going to the hospital. We're out the door before I have chance to consider researching, and the hospital's a good half-hour drive. I'm feeling hot as soon as we make it into the jeep.

Matt looks at me with concern and back to the road. I'm high, ungrounded, then stabilize for a few minutes until I get nauseous and hold my stomach, leaning out the window.

"I don't feel so good."

I'm moving from queasy to sweaty and cold.

I look at my brother; grateful he's taking care of me. I'll be fine... it doesn't burn, but I'm nauseous.

I'm deciding I won't be upset about it if I'm not going to live, but this is one lame way to die. When we finally arrive at the hospital, we tell the nurse what happened and fill out forms and they send us into a room to wait for a doctor.

I'm lying on a paper, covered bed for twenty minutes and sit up, amazed that the hospital is just going to let me die. But really I feel okay, I think, so I lay back down and contemplate my life. We'd waited an hour before the doctor finally waltzes in. He's looking over his charts and takes off his glasses, looks at my brother and I, and flatly informs us that I had eaten silicon.

"It's sand, a little gritty maybe, but inert, absolutely non-toxic." I jump off the table and look over inquisitively at Matt.

"I ate dirt! Are you serious? Why didn't you guys just tell us that when we walked in?" Then I'm realizing my antics in the jeep were psychosomatic.

"That's amazing, I'd really felt sick." I don't know whether to feel stupid or delighted.

I look at the poster of organs on the wall and back to doctor.

"Well, are we done, then?"

"Yup, you're done."

I shrug at Matt. He looks back at me, bounces his head and smiles.

"Come on, little sis," he says, and wraps an arm around me.

"I'm glad you're not dead."

"Me too." I say, smiling, looking into big brown eyes, and rest my head on his shoulder.

Matt fills out billing information, and I trot after him out of the hospital.

Climbing back into the jeep, we slide on our belts.

"Hey Matt."

"What?"

"I met a guy."

He doesn't respond beyond furrowing his brows in a perplexed 'why are you telling me that?' kind of look, turns on the ignition and shifts into reverse. There are certain subject matters Matt just doesn't want to hear about, and I just learned guys are one of them. I fold my arms and push myself back into the seat. It's too bad he doesn't want to hear about it, I really like him.

I'd met Brian on campus a few days prior. He was sitting alone on the wall with his back to me, looking over the water. He's muscular and handsome with a shaved head, a clean white tee, jeans, boots, and a guitar strapped over his shoulder. I slink over and take a seat next to him. He's got Piscean blue eyes and a mischievous grin that stretches from ear to ear.

"Brian." He reaches his hand out to me.

I think I'm in love.

He plays guitar and sings and our eyes meet for too long to be appropriate for a first meeting.

We pull up to the house. Matt and I climb up the stairs and pull our shoes off in the hall and he lets us in. Matt rolls up his sleeves and tosses himself back into his game throne. I pick up the cigarette I'd rolled earlier, and bring it out to sit in the hall. I envision kissing Brian, his hands on my body, feeling him inside of me. Smoke curls through beams of light streaming in through the upper windows of the hall.

Chapter 12 ~ Dirty Dancing

It's 5:30 am. I'm riding my bike down a quiet, foggy Texas road, crunching brown oak leaves under my tires. I pedal by barren tree skeletons. Cold air freezes my face as my breath makes tiny clouds of mist that appear, disappear.

I've been with Brian now for over two years. I've moved out of my brother's, closer to the city for our last year of University. We graduated together and decided to relocate to San Antonio so he could work at his parent's satellite office, and I could be around a community of friends. Time's moved fast, already we've been here eight months.

I remember fondly our initial meeting at University, how we'd felt so passionate, we could barely keep our hands off each other.

But we both had the same patterns in the past, driving down a road that was wild and passionate and fast. But you drive down it enough, you notice there's a lot of bodies laid out, a lot of accidents.

So we tried something new; we waited for an entire month.

The corners of my lips turn up as I pull into the gate and let myself in the shop.

A month. Big deal. Still, everything's relative- it was a leap for us.

I turn on the lights, the coffee machines, stereo.

That first time when I took him in my room had been so intense and passionate, so consumed with desire. We'd found our perfect match.

It's a while now that we've been living together, and in comparison with the passionate dramas I'd been so accustomed from the past, this relationship's been a dream come true. We'd been the best or friends, settled and stable... dispositions I'd never known or experienced.

What I can't understand is how our passions in bed went on such a downward spiral ever since that first experience, I don't know where he went.

Last night's still strong in my mind.

I crawled into bed and snuggled my body into him. He ran his fingers over me, maybe once, and pushes himself in. I'm not ready. It's way too quick. I don't want to ask him for foreplay, but it's all so dull and rushed. His eyes and lips pinched tight, he pumps away like a robot.

I searched his face; "Brian?"

He opened his eyes for a minute, kissed me, and a moment later was pumping again, his face was red and he shook before pulling out with a groan.

I've been staring at the ceiling a lot lately, wondering what's wrong. It all works fine, he's got the equipment, he's drop-dead gorgeous, any woman would want him.

But for me, I don't understand it, but there's something about the physicality of sex, in and of itself, that, even when it's good, has become unsatisfying.

Problem is, I don't really know exactly what it is that's missing.

Emotion? Intensity? Intention?

It's what I *don't feel* behind his words, his embrace, or his kiss.

It's like a force that isn't there that should be telling me he's really with me in love.

And even though I can't pinpoint what *it* actually is, without it, sex is somehow... offensive.

At the same time, I'm aware my frustrations aren't all about Brian.

After eight months of pouring over want ads, papers, and searching online, it's sinking in that the education that was supposed to be my savior, the one I worked full time through to get Summa Cum Laude, it's done nothing but put me thirty grand in debt, and as it is, I've always had trouble just making rent.

The thing is, I've followed the rules, done everything I'm supposed to, but with work, with Brian, with everything, I'm still trapped in this grip of mediocrity, more boredom, poverty... same old shit.

So when my boss, half my age, who manages this shop, the shop his parents gave him, mind you, when he looks over my shoulder that afternoon and reminds me to weigh the salami for the sandwiches- to weigh the three slices that always makes a sandwich- Every. Single.

Time, I nearly throw the toast I'm slathering with mayonnaise at his head.

I'm supposedly more sober and healthy than ever, yet I've never felt so insane.

I look around wondering how anyone can accept this dry, lifeless, godless, materially bound way of living. Laws. Wars. Presidents; This is really it?

But I have no idea what to do about it. Some ethereal drill sergeant's screaming spittle into my face twenty-four, seven: *'DO IT NOW SOLDIER!'* without the slightest inclination as to what, exactly, I'm supposed to be doing.

That afternoon I'm pedaling by the local 'Gentleman's Club,' my mind swirling in contradictions. Every day I pass this place, and every day my stomach twists in knots. The club always gets under my skin, the men, the girls, the shallow infatuation. It's all a symbolic exacerbation of the pretentious agreements that, at present, are driving me nuts.

The men place the value of their energy and focus into the fulfillment of fantasy and gratification. The women reduce themselves to seduction in order to achieve a sense of worth and freedom through economic security. It all flies in the face of the meaning and depth that I so dearly yearn for and seek. Frankly, I want to blow this s__t hole to bits.

I'm sure those girls in one night make what'd take me a week of 'honest' work. Everything about it goes against my values. I see no dignity in it.

I must admit, at the same time, the pain of my own judgment hurts just as much, in spite of its existence. At this point, doing things right and following the rules of the game seems the very nature of my imprisonment. There are so many things; I don't understand why they're here, why they exist, but being a martyr carrying the world on my shoulders makes me ponder if all this time I've been carrying my own whip.

Truth is, I'd like to be lighter, less serious, to take things in stride with less investment and personal offence. Surely I must find a way to relieve the pain of my own anguish and disgust.

So I pedal behind the club, kick my stand down, and swing open the door to the club. Late afternoon sun floods into the red light room, smoke playing through the rays while my shadow rises, condenses, disappears as the door shuts behind me. I freeze, scanning the place. Never before have I been in a strip club. The music's way too loud for three in the afternoon. Three people, two men and a scantily dressed woman in her early thirties are perched at the bar.

The girl's cute with a round face and curly brown hair, dressed only in a black leather G-string, matching top and knee-high boots. A heel is tucked into the bottom rung of her stool as she sits between two men, all of them sipping martinis and smoking cigarettes. I walk up to her and yell over the music as to where I might find management. She slides off her chair, winks with a half smirk, and touches my shoulder as she saunters down the hall.

The two men look over, and I turn away and hum along with Pink Floyd- 'Motha will they tear your little booooy APART!' I tap my foot, pretending not to notice their attention.

She returns to me, flashing green eyes between heavily mascara'd lashes.

"You fixin' to get a job?"

"I don't know, I mean... I'm not a stripper, I've never done it."

She raises her brows and grabs a cigarette from a pack on the bar.

"What's it like?' I ask.

She looks around and back to my eyes.

"Hon, you get a good thing going here, especially at night, it's the best wage around." She winks. "You're gorgeous. You won't have any trouble."

I smile in return, and watch her slide back onto her stool, cross her legs, and lean toward one of the men to light her smoke.

The manager, a man with a round, chubby face and shiny black square toe shoes comes down the hall, offers a sardonic smile and stretches out his hand:

"Chris."

"I just got a job as a stripper." I tell Brian.

The book he's reading slowly descends, blue eyes meeting mine. He grins. "You serious?"

"Yup." I sit on the couch next to him and kiss him on the cheek. "Went into that club down the street today. I hope you're ok with that. I just figured, with all the money problems I'm having and all..."

"I guess, maybe I should come in and be your body guard." He pauses.

"If anyone touches you, I kill them. Well, unless they pay you really well, that is. But you better not like it!" He giggles.

I wrap my arms around Brian. He's being way more understanding than I'd expected.

"I won't be home a lot in the evenings now."

"True," he says, "Maybe I'll start looking at a bouncing job in town. Been thinking about it, I've wanted to get out of my parents office for a while now, maybe this'll motivate me to do it."

"That'd be so good for you to get out of there."

"That it would."

The following weekend, I stride into the club, nervous but ready. Chris, clad in a navy, square-cut business suit and a red tie, finds me waiting at the bar. He slides onto a stool, runs fingers through short, brown hair, and lights a cigarette. He's got a small, sharp nose that indents at the point.

"Let's go over the rules, shall we?" he says. I nod.

"The clients aren't allowed to touch you. If they do, tell them no, and remove their hand. If they do it again, wave one of us down. We're stationed around every night. No groin contact, no drinking and no drugs during your shift."

"All the girls take turns doing a day shift. As you can see..." he opens an arm, directing me to look around the room: "...things don't really get rolling until another hour or so. Even so, the days are a good way to get better acquainted with some of the regulars. If they like you, they'll pay you well. Tonight, just have fun and blend in, you'll get the hang of things soon enough."

I look around the smoky room. A young girl with tattoos and short, elvish brown hair is on stage, her long legs spread. She's waving her ass directly in front of a man's face. He's completely fixated. Another short, stocky girl is giving a lap dance. She stands up from her client's lap, lifts a high-heeled foot onto the edge of the chair by his shoulder and opens her legs to him. It appears as if she's close to masturbating through her panties.

There's a man at the edge of the main stage. His hips are swaying side to side while he watches a girl doing tricks on the pole.

Chris leads me through a dark hallway, into a small room with mirrors for walls, and make-up counters all the way around. Girls are priming and prepping, no one so much as bats an eyelash. Chris pulls out an empty chair and motions for me to sit and get myself ready. He'll be back in twenty to send me through the rest of the process. I sit and twist open cherry red lipstick.

When Chris returns, he directs me into line behind two petite girls who look like twin sisters. They have short, curly brown hair and tan skin that sparkles, and are dressed in bikinis with twisted white and gold fringe. They're talking with the DJ on his podium. My heart's pounding. I was thinking I might get a practice run or something, but apparently, that's not how it's going.

I study the girls on stage, admiring their beauty and skills dancing with the pole and how they attend to each man that comes to them. A tall blonde climbs the pole, hangs upside down by her legs, then holds on with her hands to gracefully ease one leg, then the other down. *Right. Got it.*

I'm next.

The DJ looks down and asks my stage name. *Shit, stage name?* Shrugging my shoulders, I blurt out "Lanni Blue," and roll my eyes, *where did that come from?*

The DJ tells me I can only have one name.

"Bl..." I start, but it dawns on me, Blue alone might be asking for trouble, so then and there, I became 'Lanni.'

I request Smashing Pumpkins or old Aerosmith.   The DJ cracks a smile.

"Here for the first time on our stage tonight...beautiful, long legged, Llllanni!"

Rag Doll begins to play.

Holy shit I'm on.

I search the steps in desperation to be sure I don't trip in my heels on the way up.

I'm on stage in a red G-string and six-inch sparkling red heels that I can barely walk in.

I prance about like a shocked gazelle, turning in circles, placing my hands on my hips, and lean to the side before walking a few more steps.

Too much runway model...shit, what now?

The pole- it's behind me. I turn to take hold, but have no idea what to do, so I just walk circles around it, my free hand swinging in the breeze.

Then I turn to lean my back against it, and go sultry, sliding down until I'm seated with my legs spread a little and I reach behind and hold onto the pole and lean my head back, letting my hair fall sexy around me, and stick out my chest. Someone comes to the stage with a five-dollar bill. *Thank god!*

I get onto my knees, crawl to him, and find myself sliding around to open my legs before him, rest on my elbows, arch my neck and chest, and meet his eyes while I shake my hair out and run my hands from my inner thighs to my breasts. I lift, swing myself around to kneel by him, smile, and open the string on my hip.

He places the five, and reaches into a pocket. I shift onto my knees, run a finger under his chin, seduce him with my eyes, and turn to pull open the string on the other side, where he tucks the second five.

The DJ thanks me and introduces the next. I blow my man a kiss and get up and off stage, and amble back to the dressing room, shaking like a leaf.

I'd have several opportunities to improve that night, and many more to come, and each time I dance, I'm more comfortable being seen in my expression. That first night I went home with two hundred dollars in my pocket, more money than I'd ever made from a proper day's wage.

I'm watching Brian lumber around the house.

The longer time passes, the more my perception changes. The silence I once found mysterious and sexy now looks a lot more like numb. His calm and collected, feels more like dull and repressed. The harmony and peace between us has become lack-luster and lifeless. I think I've been waiting for something to change, as if it might, on it's own, paint itself with color and bounce into life. It all gets me to thinking.

Some five years ago, I'd lived here for a short time. The community here was vibrant and alive, something really special, it was part of our decision to move here. I'd met a man then at a New Year's gathering. He was beautiful and enigmatic and confident. He was my midnight kiss, and he'd made a strong impression on me then. Later, I came to find out, he had a wife, and in fact, she'd been there watching the entire time. It fascinated me then: how could it be possible to watch one's partner kiss another.

His name is Stephen; and he and his wife Sarah were in an open relationship.

But that's all so far out of my league. I'm not sure I'd ever be interested in something like that. But then again, I have to admit, circumstances as they are...I'm growing curious.

But thinking about Stephen and Sarah ties my mind into knots. I just don't understand it ... and that gets me considering someone else.

I had a friend that I'm sure would have some interesting things to say about all of this. In fact, I'd met him shortly after meeting Stephen. I'd never taken much interest, as he seemed like a total Gigolo, focused completely on sexuality. Still, if any one had had experience in places like this, it was this guy, and he's always invited my communication.

His name is Father Ron. He calls himself a "Tantric Sacred Sexual Healer."

I pick up the phone and dial.

"Hi honey!" he says. My shoulders drop.

"Hey Ron," I sigh, "I'm so glad you're on the other end of this line."

Ron chuckles.

"Oh honey, sounds like something's up."

I can see Ron in my minds eye, his mischievous grin and long, honey brown locks.

"It is." I say. "Got a minute to talk?"

"For you, anytime."

"Thanks Ron. Ok well," I sigh. "Actually, I don't even know how to say this."

"It's our sex life, well actually, maybe it's the relationship in general, I guess. It's just that it shows up the most in our sex life. The thing is, I get the feeling Brian thinks everything's fine as it is with us, but for me, sex with Brian feels, how do I say- mechanical? The *action*'s there and, let's say, all the plumbing works fine, but it feels like there's no *energy*, like, some intrinsic *quality is* missing, like there's no real love or passion in him. You know, it's awful to say, but it's like having sex with a robot."

"You know, I'm not even sure it's something everyone would notice, and yet to me, that quality means everything, kind of like the very juice that makes sex and love yummy, you know?"

"I just have this weird thing, like...I see, or, I guess I should say, I *feel* what's going on *behind* the scene, behind the words and the actions, you know? It's like a whole other layer, the untold story that's going on. Does that make sense?"

"Ron," I pause. "Brian bites his lip and holds his breath when we're having sex as if he's going to combust or something. If I'm totally honest, I have to say I'm just bored, because the thing that's missing, this thing I don't even know how to articulate, is like, I don't know, it feels like the source of what makes love."

"The hardest part about it is, even without knowing what it is, I'm *pining* for it."

"Am I just nuts?" I ask.

"Probably, yes," Ron responds, with a chuckle.

Before he can say any more, I'm rambling on, telling him the ideas that have been coming up:

"Maybe I'm crazy- but there's this guy named Stephen- and what do you think about polyamory? I mean...I don't know what's right. Actually, I don't really like the idea of poly. It's not how I want to live, but I have it in my head that Stephen's the key to some of my questions. All I know is if I don't figure something out soon, Ron... I'm going to lose my shit!"

Ron is cracking up.

"What!" I demand.

"Oh honey, you're ok." He says, still chuckling. Ron assures me that everything really is all right, my questions are natural, a good thing even.

He advises that I speak openly and honestly with Brian about our relationship, as well as my growing interest in Stephen.

Well there's a notion.

I like Ron's advice. It's the permission I need.

I thank Ron and let him know I'll talk with him next week.

I think I'm ready to talk with Brian about this.

Fortunately, the subject was not completely out from left field, I'd told Brian of the circumstances meeting Stephen at the onset of our relationship, regardless of holding no intention of actually doing anything about it. As for polyamory, I'd always felt it was some excuse for the sexually obsessed, so I never thought twice about it. But circumstances as they are well, yes...now I am a bit more curious.

Chapter 13 ~ The Descent

Brian glares at me. "You're telling me you want to have sex with another guy."

"That's not it!" I'm only half-lying.

"I just want us to get to know them. I want to know how they do it."

I scrunch my face and squeeze the bridge of my nose.

"I mean," I exhale. "I want to know what they're about, you know?"

Brian steadies his glare and says nothing. I look down to study the floor and gnaw my cuticles before meeting his eyes again.

"Recently, I met Stephen's wife, Sarah, in passing."

"She's," I hesitate ...

"She is *really* beautiful, Brian"

I want to vomit.

It's an understatement: she's tall with long red hair to her waist, green eyes and a perfect body. Plus she's well educated, successful, interesting, and confident enough to be in open relationship. I feel jealous just thinking about her. She's everything I'm not.

But more than my fear, I have to experience something deeper than this.

Brian runs a hand over his head.

"Let's just invite them for dinner.'"

He stares at me, juts out his chin and nods his head with his mouth open in bewilderment.

"I don't get how you're so baffled, have you not had the sense that things are, I don't know, maybe just a wee bit, dead or something?"

He blows air from his lips.

A surge of anger moves through me.

"What do you want?" he asks.

I suck in breath, trying to stay calm, but find myself glaring at him.

"I don't know Brian. Just, something...anything, besides this."

I bow, clenching my jaw. I'm being mean and unreasonable. I don't want to be. I'm not who I want to be at all.

That night I make dinner in silence. Brian's scribbling sketches in his notebook. I flip cheese and tomato sandwiches and stare into the pan; tears well and escape down my cheeks. I turn the stove off and hold onto the counter.

"I'm sorry." I say, my back to him.

We've been together for two peaceful years, the most stable relationship I've ever had. But lo and behold, I'm not satisfied, and for reasons I can't clearly define. I'm ruining us.

I lay in bed. *I've told him. Now, there's no going back.*

I walk on a muddy path, slipping over damp, mossy stones through a barren land of nothing, save the skeletons of trees. A deeper shade of grey descends and I'm in a still and silent cave. Shadows flicker across jagged, wet stone.

A warm breath brushes over my shoulders, raising the hair behind my neck. Something moves in the corner, blackness curling and turning on the floor.

On the wall, a shadow of a woman appears, and grows longer, until she steps forward into form.

She cocks her head, erratically like an insect: my heart pounds.

She's closer, dancing within a thousand shadows. Her skin is ruddy black and her eyes are red, darting about. A garland of human skulls click, clack around her neck. A belt of severed arms sways, dead and bloody from her waist.

I blink.

She's to my left, then to the right. She appears, disappears, over and over, and again... until she's upon me, bending forward, eyes rolled up so I see blood red; pupil half moons.

The heat of her breath burns into my brow, reeking of sweet blood. With each breath, inexplicable feelings of motherly love and murderous rage mix and flood through my veins and bones, shaking through me, drenching me in sweat. She pulls herself back, like a mantis about to strike, staring upward, and opens her mouth.

Her tongue lolls out, blood drips and a snake thuds onto the ground, twisting and turning around my feet. My throat closes. I want to run but it's only a thought.

Horrible red eyes roll down and look into me. I hear the whispered hiss of thousands of daemons, DEEEAHT, EEAAAHHT, AAAHGT, THAAAGT, HEEEAGT...repeating an endless mantra. My breath is pulled from my body. I'm choking, stomach clenched, gripped, blackness. I can't breathe. I can't move. Nothing comes when I try to scream.

Her eyes flicker and again roll down, looking into mine: *those are my eyes*!

"*I love you precious One*," she says: her mouth gapes, her breath erratic panting, sexual, oscillating, laughing and insane. She dances before me, undulating her hips, over-exaggerated and unnatural, a chaotic symphony of hollow bones, teeth and skulls knocking. I'm paralyzed, losing myself falling into a dream: blackness and drunken images, grunting, moaning, lines of cocaine, a thousand bodies slide oily over one another, the sound of sucking, fucking, masturbating.

A child screams, distant, alone in a blue swaddled cloth in a bag next to empty bottles in a dumpster. Kali, in the rusty distance, ravenous, searches amongst bones and ash in cremation grounds. A saddhu sits atop a corpse. It's alive, choking, struggling to get up... spitting blood.

She looks into me again and lights a flame, eyes wide, and places it deep into my belly, where it remains.

What do you want! I scream in my thoughts.

She looks at me with love and anguish:

My beloved, the tests lay ahead. Fan the flame and burn, Look away and it expires, or attain the way that forever holds the sacred fire.

Her eyes roll upwards and she screams as if being burning alive. The sound travels from all around: everywhere. An owl's wing and feathers batter me. Its head turns, massive, knowing yellow eyes. Talons scratch at my face. I grab at my head, covering my eyes and ears, trying to scream. There is nothing but her terrible scream; *is that me?* Darkness rises, crawling up lungs and neck, through my chin and face, filling my ears. I am on my stomach. I lift my head, gasping for air. Awake.

I lay there, heart thumping, *A dream... thank God, just a dream.*

Brian's silhouette breathes silent in the dark. Shaken, I wrap my arm around him and press my body up close.

Father Ron's name is on my cell ID.

"Hi honey!" He always sounds so excited.

"Hey Ron, how are you? What's up?"

Ron tells me he's in Hawaii. Over the past few weeks, he's been traveling through California giving workshops and talks, and just arrived this morning on Big I.

"Sounds nice." Translation: I'm jealous.

"I feel really blessed, honey. Tell me, how are things with Brian?"

"I don't really know for sure. He was upset when I first brought up the Stephen and Sarah thing, but yesterday he met up with Sarah for lunch. It was their first time meeting." I giggle.

"Funny, he seems to have lightened up a bit since then."

Ron chuckles.

"Yes...interesting."

"I'm seeing Stephen tomorrow. I'm excited."

"That sounds fun."

"Well, it's just lunch...but yeah."

"And what about the club?"

"You know Ron, I have to admit; the men in there just aren't the monsters I'd expected. There are always the bachelor parties, and that's usually the young and dumb ones getting drunk and obnoxious, they don't get the rules of the exchange, but that's really as bad as it gets.

The rest tend to be more regulars, and they're the ones I get to spend some time with.

Really, they're just lonely men. I think this is the only place where some of them get any kind of and attention.

So in that way, I can see where there's some benefit to the place.

And you know, against everything I'd expected, in the beginning, the club was kind of therapeutic."

"Really? How so, love?" Ron asks.

"Well, there's the obvious thing of the money, but what's surprised me is I've liked the exchange of it, it's clean and honest.

It's actually been relieving to interact with the men without all the strings, and attachments.

In real life, the men have always gone after me for sex."

"You're hot, honey. I'm sure they have."

"Well, it's nice when it's wanted, but truth is, it's been such a constant, I don't know how to trust men. The pull is always there. I feel some weird guilt that I'm supposed to give more of myself just for talking to a man.

But dancing's a kind of permission.

I get to be beautiful and sexy and express myself, and there's no pressure or guilt or obligation to give more for being that.

In the club, at least I'm given something back through their dollars. There's some respect and honor given back to me, rather than this thing I always must pull back from because I'm not here just for the taking. This way I get to play.

The exchange of it makes me feel more seen and appreciated. It's direct feedback, and it's given me more confidence. I've felt myself walking taller, and not just from the heels."

We both laugh.

"I think there's one more thing I should say about the club."

"Shoot."

"Well, considering my past, it's a no, brainer that I should have given more consideration to the environment I was placing myself in.

I just went for it. I was on a mission.

Frankly, all the drinking and smoking reeks and it's gross to be around if I don't participate in it, but at this point, even one or two drinks a night really messes me up, and the club's always full of smoke. My body can't handle it.

I've tried dancing sober a bunch of times, but I always make less money, much less, and then, what's the point of my being there at all.

Truth is, I don't mean to sound snobbish, but I just don't want to be in that environment. It's all of my past that I want to be done with.

Besides that, you know, I've been living off of my looks all of my life.

I desire for men to see me as a person, not just a walking sex object.

I know I'm *more* than this. I feel that I have a purpose and talents. I just want to have the space and the means to find them."

"I hear you honey, maybe we'll talk more about that soon." Ron says.

"Ron, I'd really like that."

"Meanwhile, I'm not sure what to do. I've finally got some financial security and freedom, but I can't keep it up there. I'm totally exhausted."

"Be the Goddess," he said.

"Go back to work... and this time, be the Goddess."

"Be the Goddess," I repeat.

I imagine Kali on stage, black skinned in heels and g-string with a garland of skulls around her neck and a belt of men's arms dangling from her waist. She's holding a pink lotus in one hand and a sword in the other. She flashes her wild eyes and grins, lifts her sword, pulls it back and swings it through the crowd of men standing at the edge of the stage. Heads fall, one after the other, from shoulders, to drop and go rolling onto the floor...

"You there?" Ron asks.

"Uh...ya. Sorry, I was a little distracted."

"What, exactly, does that mean, be the Goddess?"

"Embody the Goddess," Ron instructs. "Be in your power when you're up there."

I don't really understand what 'being in my power' means either.

But I'm already feeling more hopeful.

I'm sitting next to Sarah in her car. I can't hold the question back any longer: "Sarah...how do you do it, I mean, how do you share Stephen?"

She looks ahead at the road; her manicured hands steady on the wheel.

"Stephen's an extremely sexual man," she says, shrugging her shoulders. "Who am I to ask him not to be?"

I turn to watch the trees and long grasses as we pass.

I have more questions, but I don't feel right to dig further just yet.

Is there something wrong with their sex life? Why would being with her alone be asking him not to be extremely sexual? Why isn't their relationship enough?

I can't decide if it's truly as simple as she's putting it right now, or if I'm just too insecure and attached to believe that open relationship might be a more conscious and loving path?

I'm drunk on red wine, and for quite some time, I'd forgotten all about Brian. Stephen and I are sitting on the thick, beige carpet beside his bed. He leans down on his elbow and tips his head, following me with curious, steely blue eyes. Taking my hand into his, he closes his eyes, presses my palm to his lips, and breathes in the scent of my skin.

Stephen's everything I aspire to be: a traveler, a writer, passionate, brilliant, and open. I want to know this will work, that life never has to be a monotonous bore, that we could all fall in love and enjoy our lives together. I'm not completely sure I'd *always* want them to be with us ... and I definitely wouldn't want anything more than this on either end. It's about more love, not just more sex, isn't it? I don't know if they feel the same, maybe they're more open than I'm comfortable with.

Stephen leans in, "What's going on in that head of yours?"

I meet his eyes, exhale, and run my fingers through blonde locks that run down to his shoulders, and tuck a bit behind his ear.

I'm already here, and I won't truly know what's real unless I give this an honest chance. I lean into him, and taste the merlot on his breath, then his lips and tongue.

I hear a groan.

Suddenly my dreamy fog grows thick and heavy, and my heart throbs. I rise from my seat to look over the bed.

It's Brian. Sarah's straddled on top of him, moving on him. His cock is thrusting in and out of her.

"No, Brian...*WAIT!*"

I reach my hand across the bed. He meets my eyes and reaches to me. Sarah stops, straddled with him inside her. Brian and I clasp hands and hold each other's gaze.

I'm naked on every level, and suddenly, acutely aware of it. I let go of Brian's hand, grab a blanket from the end of the bed, run from the bedroom, and throw myself on the couch, sobbing. A concerned Stephen follows after me, soon followed by Sarah and Brian. Stephen sits beside me, running fingers through my hair, explaining that everything, *really*, is all right: this is a natural reaction.

I don't believe him. Surely I'm ridiculous, I initiated all of this...and I was so concerned about hesitant Brian. But no worries; he's fine- didn't even have a moment to ask me if I was ready to go all the way with this.

As usual -as always- I'm an emotional basket case.

I thought this was what I wanted, but is it? Really...what are we doing?

Soft leather reins slide between my fingers while I slow the beast cantering beneath my seat when Stephen takes me riding on Indian willow trails.

"You're the one." He says, tipping his head as if surprising himself with the thought as he trots up beside me with a delighted grin. He takes my hand. His gold wedding band is handsome on his finger. I pretend I hadn't heard those three words. There's too many questions, but for now, I just want to set them aside, allow them to pass, and trust the feeling there's something extraordinary and unique between us, some ethereal contract written thousands of lifetimes prior.

Chapter 14 ~ May 9, 2005

It's my thirty-third birthday. My Mom arrived into San Antonio early this morning.

I'm watching her having a great time with Brian and Stephen and Sarah, sitting in the backyard, sipping wine under the stars. She pulls her long silver hair behind an ear and smiles, her head tipped sideways at Brian.

For all that she's accepting, between my love life and most recent occupation, this is the first time I've ever felt genuine respect for the woman.

Brian grins and bursts out laughing, followed by Stephen and Sarah.

I have to admit, we've been happier and more content together since Stephen and Sarah came into our lives. It's alive and vibrant, full of movement and experience.

It's all so surreal: I don't know the subtleties and quirks, the humanness that I'm accustomed to with lovers, their lives, their thoughts, emotions and concerns are so separate and distant from ours.

Perhaps, by bringing us all together here with my mom, the foundation of our relationships will be solidified, it'll somehow qualify and substantiate us, make it all feel more real.

I barely noticed my mom excuse herself. A few minutes later, I hear my name. I turn.

My mother's standing in the kitchen, sunken and pale, motioning me inside.

She just got off the phone. She was just speaking with a doctor on the east coast.

"It's Matt. He's in the hospital."

Her eyes search mine.

"The doctor said he's in really bad condition."

"What do you mean...how bad?"

I don't hear her response.

I watch her dial the phone. She says she's looking for emergency flights home.

I stand there, staring.

These things are always over-exaggerated, I decide, and go out to the back yard, pick up my wine, meet eyes with Stephen and Sarah, and hear myself explaining:

"A few hours ago, my brother had a brain aneurism. The doctor said he's in a coma."

I sit and take my wine glass in both hands, look in the distance, and sip.

"But, I'm sure he'll be fine."

Actually, I can really see the perfection in it. Surely, this is just the kind of wake up call he needs to get back on track.

I get up and pace and explain.

"He'd been working for a while for Verizon, working way too much." I shake my head, gesturing with my hands. "Even more, he'd just begun his American dream: this year he bought a house, a jeep, motorcycle...he even got a dog."

"He's wanted a family more than anything, but I don't know how he's planning on creating a family when all he does is work and drink coffee and beer and play video games. He definitely hasn't been happy."

I rub my chin, shaking my head in the wisdom of it all; yes, surely this is just what he needs to snap out of it.

My wine's rippling in the glass. I put it down, assuring them again, it's ok, really, there's nothing to worry about.

Brian shows up behind me and takes my hand and I grab my wine and he walks me into the house and sits me down at the table next to my mom. I tap my fingers and get up to refill my glass and pace one room to the other. My mom's talking on the phone trying to get more details from someone. Brian pulls out his computer, suggesting he'll research flights. I agree and sit next to him and stare at the screen for a second and get back up to go outside again and take a few more sips of wine and explain the rest of the situation:

"Matt's been under a lot of stress lately, this is all perfectly understandable: he was planning on getting married to a woman he hardly knew.

They'd been together for only a month, and they got pregnant.

The girl's mother is a devout Christian, and she'd given Matt an ultimatum: she demanded the two be wed, and if he didn't, she told him he wouldn't be allowed to participate in the child's upbringing.

For Matt, it's a damn nightmare, because it's all sent him crashing into his own immovable moral code. I haven't even thought about it all that much until now, but he must be so stressed out. This really does make a lot of sense.

See, Matt handled being abandoned by our father a little different than I did. He hates our dad, and any man who leaves his children, for that matter. And now, he's got to face this decision to either marry a woman he hardly knows, and place all he's just beginning to gain into jeopardy, or he's forced to abandon his own child. Initially he'd agreed to the marriage. But when he announced it to the family a few moths ago, none of us held back our concerns. A few weeks later, he told me he could see the logic and changed his mind.

Still, no matter which way he goes, it hits too close to home. How's he going to go against his own rules, you know?

Not only that, but the very thing he's always wanted is happening and he's not welcome to be a part of it. The mother's not at all being fair to him"

I look up and realize I'm pacing.

"I better see what's going on."

I get up and go inside to stand next to my mother on the phone, trying to catch wind further on the situation. She hands the phone over. It's Matt's best friend since he was sixteen, Chris, who's now also his roommate. He pleads with me through my assured disavowal: "He's in a coma, but he's gone. His heart's beating, but only because he's being kept alive on machines."

He'd seen the x-rays of Matt's brain.

"Laurel... He's not coming back." He sobs, "The inside of his head looks like a fucking bomb exploded!"

I'm not convinced.

Those are intense words, but it's *Matt*; *of course* he'll wake up!

I remind my mom and Brian that he'll be fine.   This is all being exaggerated.

Stephen and Sara stay for just the appropriate length of time in a circumstance such as this, and as I watch them depart, Chris' words loop in my head:

"Like a fucking bomb exploded."

As we land, I call my father who I haven't spoken to since the summer of my visit. When he answers, I inform him that his son is dying, and if he cared to see him, he's at the Leonard Memorial. I hang up the phone.

When we are finally allowed entrance into my brother's room, I'm plunged into some surreal Stanley Kubrick scene.

I follow a white coat to the bed.

Matt's full of tubes, a large one in his mouth and two up his nose. The sound of respiration, in between mechanical clicks, permeates the room.

His curls cascade over naked shoulders, more frail than I last remember, and his top lip is swelled out like a duck's bill.

The doctor explains that Matt is brain dead. He opens his right lid and shines a flashlight into his eye.

"No pupil response." He says.

I lean in closely, distrustful, but he's right, there's no sign of response.

"His body is only alive due to the machines. We were awaiting your arrival so we can proceed to turn off the machines and pronounce his death. We'll need to stay and make arrangements with them. They'll be harvesting his organs per his instructions on his license."

"I'm sorry," the doctor says. "Please, take your time. I'll check back in about an hour."

I stare at my brother. Tears stream down my face. I still can't believe this is happening.

My father walks in. I hug him, not knowing what else to do, and watch him watching his dying son. He stayed there in the middle of the room and stood silent, until a tear fell down his cheek. I soften.

For several hours, friends and old lovers faded in and out. My mother and Chris and I all take turns stroking his hands and forehead, and speaking with him through our tears, letting him know he was loved and that it was safe for him to go. I braid a lock of his long hair, to cut and hold with me. Mid-way through, I remember a secret from when Chris and Matt were teenagers. They'd been in such a huff: Chris took Matt's toothbrush and scrubbed the toilet seat with it. It was so deceptive, I never forgot, and I never ratted; it would have started a war way beyond what had already been, and really, each other was all they had. I shoot Chris a look and sign language; 'toothbrush' the way we used to so many years ago. Through our tears we burst out laughing.

Chapter 15 ~ The Ides of Change

After returning home to San Antonio, I go through the paces, working the club enough to get by, and return home only to become a fixture in the living room.

Miraculously, Brian's somehow managed to become even more emotionally distant. At this point, I'd like to sink into my depression and die, like any self-respecting normal human being might do.

But instead, this fire burns in my belly, and I don't know what it wants: the blood and guts of feeling and emotion? Wild, intense passions, respect, honor...someone to take the reins? Nurturing, gentle, intimate love, their unfathomable combination in a live-flesh man to experience life and love with? God? *What*?

I don't know, but apparently this thing in me has no sympathy, and it's gotten a hold of bellows.

Months pass until I'm bored and tired of being bored and tired. I call Stephen and Sarah.

That night, I look up to find Stephen pressed against the screen door. He bounds in my direction, shooting Brian a passing greeting; "I know you understand." he says, and kneels down besides me to meet me with zealous kisses.

Sara followed in to meet with Brian, but I barely caught a glimpse before Stephen was leading me by the hand and we were in the shower. The contrast of the expression of Stephen to the state I'm in is rain in a desert. We make love more passionately than ever, madly, eagerly we love each other...aching, moaning, fully immersed within the passion and ecstasy of our love.

When the time came when we began to land back onto the planet, in a shower, in my apartment, we pause, and without a word, break into laughter from the absurdity of our love and pleasure.

I tussle Stephen's damp hair with a towel and dry his body while he grins like a contented child. Slithering back into our clothes, we stumble out to join Brian and Sarah, and stop in our tracks. They're on the couch,

Sarah sitting up in her skirt and a bra with Brian, fully dressed, lying with his head rested in her lap. She's stroking his forehead, comforting him. She looks to us, raises her brows and apologetically shrugs her shoulders.

A wave of guilt courses through me. I hadn't held back the sounds of my pleasure in the least. It had been too long since I'd lost myself, and God only knows how long we'd been going on like that in the shower. Remembering how those feelings were for me, I can only imagine how it was for Brian to just lie there and listen.

Lately, he barely talks to me. I rarely see him feeling anything at all.

A few days later I'm sitting down with Stephen: the point, I explain, of our experimenting together was to try and find a way to work things out with Brian, not pull us further apart, but Brian's been even more distant as of late.

"Stephen, I have to end this relationship with you and Sarah now."

"What... Why?"

I go silent.

"I just can't do this anymore. I don't understand what's going on for Brian. I thought he didn't care any more, but then he was a mess the other day on the couch. I just have to give this one last try."

Stephen's eyes dart and he opens his palms.

"But it's more than Brian." I say, "I mean, really, I don't know how to say this." I sigh and look down at my hands. "Stephen, it's just that, you're just too sexual for me."

Stephen's head jerks back.

"I'm too sexual?"

He jumps up and paces, shaking his head.

"What are you talking about?" His palms fly open, "*I'm* too sexual!"

"I don't know, I just...I want Brian and I to work out, I thought this would make things different somehow."

"Things *have* been different, Laurel!" I still love the way he says my name, even when he's mad.

"I know...I mean...Stephen," now I'm getting heated, "it's just that, every single time, we're always drinking wine and so focused on sex, and I just need something different than that."

"What! You love the sex too!"

"Stephen...I do." I sigh, dropping my head into my hands.

"It's more about emotion or intimacy or something. You know, what's been going on is beautiful; I've loved all of our experience. It's just that, I don't know, there's just something more I have to find, and I don't really understand what it is. I know this sounds ridiculous. I'm sorry for that. I don't know what else to do, Stephen. I love you, but I just have to end this."

A week later, Brian and I agree it's better we be friends. We still want to support each other, but our time has come. I'll put a futon in the office and we'll be roommates until I find another place.

I'm in bed flipping through a book on an American Buddhist's journey and I find a slip of paper between the pages on which I'd jotted a note:

Revulsion for Samsara: a feeling of revulsion for the absurdity of one's own life. It is the impetus for change and the foundation of one's personal journey.

That sounds about right.

My cell rings.

I fold the paper and tuck it back between the pages, place the book on the bedside table and grab my phone. It's Ron.

He asks me how I am, and I blurt out everything.

I tell him I ended things with Stephen and Sarah, and then with Brian.

"Ron. I'm just going to say this, even though it doesn't make any sense."

"I am all ears."

"I have two beautiful men available to me if I want, but I don't want to be with either of them. I'm sure there are circumstances when that's perfectly normal, but the thing is Ron, I'm on fire, totally turned on, but I don't want to have sex with either of them. It doesn't make any sense. They're both gorgeous, they're awesome, actually, but it's the sex, even though I've never had sexual issues, minus my bore with Brian...it's always been orgasmic and all of that.

I don't know Ron, it's just missing something, no matter how good it is, it's not ultimately satisfying, and I don't really know what will be; maybe deeper emotion or intimacy, I'm not sure. It's like, I'm dying to be met in my intensity, ravaged even, but not just sexually... more emotionally? I don't know... could it be Spiritually?" I sigh, feeling unable to communicate this accurately.

"Honey, I hear you. You're frustrated, huh."

I lighten.

"Totally! I have no idea what to do. I think most women would die to be in my shoes. But honestly, there's something so, I don't know, boring, even offensive about sex as normal people do it, no matter how good. Isn't that weird? I actually think that this might not even be about sex. Maybe what I yearn for is unattainable. I feel like I need to go to an Ashram or something."

"And just to make things harder, it feels like the club is sucking the life from me. I've been coming home every night more sick and exhausted. I want to leave, but I can't go back to a deli job. That will kill me. I don't know what else to do. Basically, I'm a mess all around. Isn't that lovely? Hi Ron, and how are you?"

Ron reminds me that he thinks I'm someone very special. He's always told me that. In fact, he's sure I'm a Tantric, a Dakini as he calls it. He knows me, he says. I've been training all of my life for this. It's even written in my name.

He's told me that before. Actually, it's something I've heard more than once.

I remember my mother once had a yogi boyfriend.

He was driving my mom and I to the movies, and he looked into the rearview and randomly asked me if I knew the meaning of my last name.

"All I know," I told him, "is it was a longer Lithuanian name once, but it got shorted when my grandparents on my father's side got off the boat into America. That's about it."

"Yoni," he told me, "means ...vagina."

I shrink in the back seat and my eyes slide to the side.

"But it's much more than that," he said, "Yoni represents the Mother, where all things are derived from. The Mother, basically, is everything that is form, really all that is."

I sit back up.

"Ka," he continues, "means the Great Spirit."

He told me the name is very Tantric. It means that I am the Great Spirit of Yoni.

I raised a brow and told him I thought that was a little lofty and let it go at that.

"I think this is your calling." Ron says.

"Laurel, what if we were to travel the world and teach Tantra together?"

I yank the phone from my ear, glaring at it.

"Wow." I try not to act as shocked as I am. "I'd love that, but what do you mean? How? I don't know a thing about Tantra."

"Laurel, Come to the temple. I'll be there in a few weeks. Let's see what's possible, what we might create together. I've been waiting long enough for you."

He says more, but my mind's spinning, so I tell him I'll think about what he's saying and hang up the phone.

Travel the world to teach with him? He can't be serious.

He's always expressed his interest, but he's a player. Every time we speak he's with a different woman, so I've never given a second thought to his advances.

But it would be so cool to travel and teach! I don't get how, but he's inviting me, and my past *has* been highly sexual. Maybe Ron's right. Maybe this is my destiny. Maybe I'm supposed to become a Dakini; a Tantric Sexual Healer.

Chapter 16 ~ Tantric Temple Life

I catch a shuttle bus out of Albuquerque, where cement buildings and high walls along the highway turn to dusty grasslands and tall saguaro. When we reach the forested outskirts of Santa Fe, the landscape drastically shifts. The sun sets, splashing warm rays across majestic red rock spires that stretch to the heavens. Ghost images of native warriors riding painted ponies in full gallop dances through my veins.

125 Kokopelli Drive. I confirm the address I'd marked on a tattered business card with the mailbox the driver just pulled next to.

"This is it!"

I hop down the stairs to pull out my bags. I thank the driver, hand him a tip, and lift my bag over the gravel driveway leading to a cedar fence bordered in rosemary. I knock but there's no reply, so lift the metal latch and peek my head in the gate to a smooth stone entranceway to the house, with fish ponds bordered by rock, cedar and aspen. In the center: a trickling Shiva lingam.

Carved maple doors open to a woman with warm, brown eyes and a soft smile.

"Welcome. You must be Laurel."

She takes my hand and gestures me in, tips her head and opens her arms to embrace.

"Hi. My name's Brenda," she says as our bodies peel apart.

"Make yourself comfortable." She nods towards a couch at the entrance.

"I'll let Ron know you're here."

As she walks toward a small office in the corner, I sense something was peculiar in her greeting, I'm curious if she's Ron's lover.

I set my bags down and take in an impressive, thickly carpeted room with rose wine walls and high, fanned ceilings. Massive, sliding glass doors open the back of the house to a panoramic view of desert grasslands, flanked by stunning red rock mountains. Burgundy velvet curtains frame the landscape, held by golden ties, and over-sized cream pillows wait invitingly before a stone hearth framed with hanging candelabras and a giant statue of Buddha, meditating to the side. A quarter of the room by the office is kitchen space; divided by a grand, black granite countertop and bamboo flooring.

Ron appears from a side entrance door, lifts his shoulders to his ears, and tiptoes over. He wraps me into his arms and fills his belly with air only to sigh it out, swaying us side to side before pulling back. He takes me by the shoulders, and we meet each other's eyes, grinning ear to ear.

"I am so happy you're here, Goddess"

'I'... *Goddess*?

My eyes travel across the floor.

"It's, um, good to be here." I escape his glance and turn my attention on the room.

"This is a really a beautiful home, Ron!'

"Well, it's yours to enjoy for a while!' Shall I show you around?"

He opens the side door.

"I'm sure you're tired from your trip, we can go in the back and snuggle afterwards, if you like." he says, gesturing his hand toward a long corridor. "Miss Yoni-*ka*!"

"There's six bedrooms in all," he says, and opens the first of four doors along the length of the hall.

I peek into a moderately sized room with saffron walls, with its own bathroom and a walk-in closet, deep-orange curtains and a matching bedcover. The other three rooms are similar, although each one is decorated in its own unique color and theme. We continue through a door at the end of the hall that opens into a humid greenhouse filled with banana trees and potted plants. A fountain trickles water down smooth stones inlayed into the east corner wall, and to the right is an open door to a steam room, with sliding glass doors that open to a hot tub, watsu, and a saltwater cold pool.

"Use them whenever you like!"

We walk through to the opposite side, where glass double doors open to a second grand room with two giant, raw cut beams of Juniper that twist floor to ceiling at each end of the room. A wood-burning stove is nestled into the left hand corner, and oversize pillows are stacked before a grand theatre screen.

"We'll snuggle and watch movies there." Ron says, grinning and toggling his head. Beside the screen is a long, maple wood desk displaying flyers, stacks of business cards, books and CDs on Tantra and Sacred Sex, lubrications, condoms, and sex toys of every shape, size, and color. I pick up a translucent, L-shaped toy with a bulb on the end, curious as to its ergonomic purpose. Ron takes my hand and opens a door behind the desk.

"This is the master bedroom," he says, gesturing me in, and opens curtains to a view of the Shiva lingam fountain just outside the window. He then rolls onto his giant bed covered with feather pillows, holds out his arms, and wiggles his fingers.

"Come snuggle," he coos.

We lay there, eyes meeting. He's so excited I've come to be part of the Temple staff and family. He'll be traveling in and out over the next few weeks, but when he's home, he'd like us to spend as much time together as possible.

Sessions are always happening at the temple. There's a talk on Wednesday, and a workshop next week. He'd like me to attend.

"Soon enough, you'll be giving sessions of your own!"

I swallow. *Soon?*

He tucks my hair behind an ear.

"You are so beautiful, Goddess."

I shrink, looking away. It's sinking in that I've just moved into a mansion and signed my life over to some unspoken Poly-tantric contract with this man.

That evening, Ron and I made love for the first time. He moved confidently, sliding his hands over my body as if he's touched me a thousand times, our tongues tasting each other's lips. He kisses my breast and rolling his tongue along the darker, soft flesh, brushes his fingers along the inside of my thigh, and over the damp, pink flesh of my sex.

But something's off about his movement as he caresses and kisses my belly.

He pauses.

"No." he whispers, nodding his head and a tear runs down his face.

I loop my hand under his shoulder and ask him to stop.

"What's going on for you?" I ask, but he doesn't respond.

I urge him back up, assuring him. He'd initiated. I thought it was what he wanted, but by no means do we need to do this. I try assuring him again, but he continues, going down to my yoni, he licks, slow and gentle, again and over again, before a pause. He breathes in deep, as if savoring my essence, and looks up.

"Goddess," he says, "the smell of you, the taste of you, is absolutely divine."

Apparently, he loves to pleasure me, so I do my best to relax and let whatever just happened go and enjoy him. He brings me to orgasm several times, lifts his eyes again to mine, raises himself up, and makes love to me for the first time.

We sink deep into each other until the delicious intensity of our pleasure meets its highest peak, and there he stops movement, sits up, and takes in an exaggerated breath. We play along an exquisite edge, resuming and pausing, enjoying the bliss of no movement at all, remaining in control within our heightened senses, until his intensity grows too high to continue, and he lay me down to pleasure me again and again.

Wobbly and spent, we wrap ourselves within each other's arms and drift into darkness, remaining there in deep sleep without a stir until the morning when I dream: a grey and dark blanket of clouds illuminates, orange and pink slowly painting color into the distance. The misty skies part, and there a rainbow appears, dim at first, then growing moment by moment into bright, double arches, one above the other, stretching full, a vivid glory over green, lush lands.

The rising sun pushes thin beams of light between the long, vertical blinds in Ron's room that grow long across the thick carpet, climb along the side of our bed, and warm our faces. Ron's strong arms wrapped around me, I'm immersed in the decadence of thick, feather blankets and fluffy pillows, alchemized with the dream's vision: heaven and earth meet, transforming our love into the realms of the Divine.

The dream is my omen. I'll remain with him until my time is done.

Right away, I'm fully immersed into life in a Tantric Temple, and until I bring in income from sessions, I'll have chores to contribute as rent of sorts. There are rooms to clean, windows to wash and pools and water systems that need to be checked, as well as work at the front desk: sessions to schedule, data entry and research, advertising, and meetings to coordinate with the Temple Dakas and Dakinis, which I'm finding out, is akin to herding cats.

Our mission, I am told, is to create an abundant and sustainable Tantric Sacred Sexual Temple.

Soft orange firelight softens Ron's honey locks as he addresses a small circle of women in the Temple's den.

"Most people have lots of shame, guilt, and fear around sex," Ron says "it's the very root of resentment and separation between men and women. From the first day we're borne, our parents, schools, media, and our culture paints pictures for us about what our sexual and relational lives should look like. When we were young and exploring our bodies, most of our parents either avoided the subject, or shamed and punished us. For example, little boys often learn early on that masturbation is shameful, and learn to be secretive and masturbate quickly so they won't get caught. It conditions them into a pattern of fast paced, physical sex connected with fear and shame that they carry into their adult lives.

Girls commonly get very little or no information around sex or pregnancy. They often are given the idea that if they desire sex out of marriage, they're somehow impure or dirty. They often don't understand their anatomy, their monthly cycles, or how to deal with virginity, and from the contradicting messages within the culture, they're pressured to somehow become both the Madonna and the whore.

Even her own peers, all of them conditioned more or less along similar lines, act to reinforce her insecurity and confusion.

So in a nutshell, most of us started, to one degree or another, conditioned towards sex as dirty, shameful, and impure, and something that is only allowed in either marriage or a monogamous relationship.

Then the picture looks something like: you go to school, get a job, get married, and then work your whole life until you get a pension and then, if you're really lucky you're respected and taken care of as an elder, but more likely, you're sent off to an old folks home, and then you die! Doesn't sound all that fun, right?"

We all look at each other and laugh. His words are music to my ears.

"And it's not! There are parts of us that we bring into this world that don't agree with this picture. You might have sexual tendencies other than monogamy, or little interest in marriage, or raising a family."

"You might have spiritual abilities or creative talents that are at odds with social norms. Early on, we learn to repress those qualities, because if we acted out on them, our parents, friends or institutions would tell us we were wrong, or bad, or punish us, or we might even be sent to jail if we were to express our unique individual selves. Those qualities don't just go away, they're still there, but what happens when these aspects are denied or repressed, is they eventually will arise from the unconscious in one way or another. If it's completely ignored or denied, it might show up as a mental issue or a chronic or life threatening disease. Sexual repression often arises in a distorted form that is destructive. The recent sex scandals that have popped up everywhere of Catholic priests molesting young boys, for example. This isn't a sudden, new phenomenon. It's just that the information's coming out now."

"So one of the most common ways this happens is that when something is too scary or shameful according to the culture, and we become unable or unwilling to see it within ourselves, it becomes self-denial. Then the only way we see it is by projecting the denied or repressed aspect onto others. When we're projecting our own stuff onto others, it's going to show up, a lot, and most often, it will have a strong emotional trigger attached of either attraction or repulsion, depending on if the repressed aspect is a quality we like, or dislike. Everything we fear and deny will perpetually show up in our face. We're here to learn. That is the nature of this life."

"Self-denial and projection creates judgment, meaning we make others wrong. What we are doing then is boosting our own ego by making ourselves 'right'. 'They are like this. I'm not.' 'They do this, I don't,' and that judgment is what creates fear, hatred and separation. So when we carry with us our sexual denial and repressions, this is why we have so much difficulty in marriage and our relationships. We can't see our own dysfunctions, and we become confused and contradicted, and go into lying and cheating and sneaking. We don't know our true nature, especially as sexual beings."

Ron meets the eyes of each woman in the circle, nodding his head.

"So this is where our inner work gets really interesting, and there's an initiative, a carrot, let's say," he lifts his hand to his chest.

"What happens is, our greatest gifts and talents are hidden behind those fears and judgments. It's precisely where we find the gems, our highest creative potential.

In order to break through judgment and unbury our greatest gifts, we need to be ruthless with ourselves, by understanding that: to the degree that we judge something outside of ourselves, is to the degree that aspect is hidden and repressed within our own mind and body. The key to remember is, the repressions and denied aspects will express themselves through the emotional signposts of attraction and repulsion. The intense emotions are the energies that are trying to get our attention, and it does!"

Ron chuckles, "It's extremely effective!"

Ron's smile is beautiful as he pauses. The truth in his words makes me feel proud to sit next to him. But some of the other women are clearly placing him on a pedestal, sinking into their seats, their eyes smoldering. Ron seems to eat it up, returning their gazes with adoration.

"Tantra teaches us to turn and embrace all that is: to follow our desires and face our fears and our judgments. When we own these parts of ourselves, and bring our shadows to light, our nervous system gets to relax, we get to enjoy pleasure and end the resentment and separation. It's our birthright as conscious, vibrant and alive sexual beings on the planet. This is where we polish our link to the Divine!"

I get to polish our link tonight.

Ron places a hand on his belly.

"Now, women in particular carry a lot of pain and trauma in their wombs. The key to healing these wounds and opening women to their full orgasmic potential is through an ancient Tantric practice called sacred spot massage."

Ron and I have been practicing sacred spot several times a day before we make love. He sits between my legs and massages my Yoni with his fingers and tongue, then requests to enter my 'sacred temple' with his fingers. He never seems to tire of it or be in a rush. He loves to make me come before we make love.

I ask, "Is there a sacred spot for men?" If I'm going to be a Dakini, I want to know everything as quickly as possible.

"Yup. Actually, a man's sacred spot is his prostate."

I pause. My eyes widen.

"Wait. You mean..." I hold my palm up, gesturing with my index finger without fully realizing I'm doing it.

"That's right, the prostate is accessed through a man's anus. A Dakini will perform sacred spot on her client and this is an extremely beautiful and vulnerable experience for a man to feel what it's like to be penetrated. Most men absolutely love it!"

My eyes glaze over as the information settles in.

Seriously, I'm going to be massaging men through their anus?

"When the wounded places in the sex centers of the physical body are touched and loved through sacred spot massage, the Tantric practitioner holds the space for the emotional backlog of pain and trauma to arise and be healed. Many women are so hurt and afraid around sex, they've never been able to experience the pleasure of orgasm. Through sacred spot, women can retrain their bodies so their amrita, the female ejaculate, can flow once again. When the women are flowing their amrita, they're happy and can once again stand in their power. If the women are in their power, then the rivers will once again flow freely, and pollution and destruction of the planet will end. In order for that to happen, we have to let go of the guilt, shame and fear around sex."

Ron pauses and takes a deep breath.

"When you have sexual freedom," he nods his head, "you become the Goddess."

Ron pulls the corners of his lips back, and pauses to gaze, one by one, into the eyes of each woman in the circle. Sometimes he nods, or pushes his chest forward lets out a dreamy sigh.

Ron's ideals inspire and excite me to gain a deeper understanding of Tantra and learn the art of becoming a Sacred Sexual healer. Even when I'm gathering my things at the end of the talk along with the group, some of the women are looking upon him with eyes shining wide like animated bunnies while he acknowledges them. Several of them wait to speak with him as he opens his schedule book. He's got two sessions scheduled for tonight, and the others are lining up for later in the week.

I could swear I'm watching Ron's sexual enticement for these women. But they're clients. Is that ethical? But he's been doing this over twenty years. It's his expertise. What do I know? Still, as true as his words are, I know what I'm seeing and I'm seriously questioning his integrity. I suppose I've always questioned him when it comes to women, but clients are a different story. Still, just as Ron says, what if this is my projection, my distorted perspective, my guilt, shame and fear from sexual conditioning?

Chapter 17 ~ Memories

It's Sunday morning under clear blue New Mexico skies. Ron, myself, and two of his cousins crawled from our beds early to take a challenging trek up Jemez Mountain, just behind the temple. We've been at a fast pace for two hours along the steep, rocky trail interspersed with prickly pear cactus and twisting juniper. Five or six ravens circle, cawing above. Red hills and canyons spread to the horizon in every direction. Mystical red rock spires splashed with morning light rise toward the skies.

Not far from the peak, we come upon an exposed cliff edge, perhaps a foot and a half wide, but no more than a six or seven foot traverse, to the other side. The boys easily step across with me in tow. But half way across, I look over the steep abyss. Gasping, I shove my body against rock and claw between cactus spikes for any vegetation to grab onto for dear life. Fingers taught on tiny clumps of dry grass, I freeze, panting against the rock.

A hand reaches out to me. I look up to meet Ron's cousin Jason's green eyes.

"Laurel"

"Look at me. Take my hand." He motions with his fingers.

"You're safe. I'll get you across."

My eyes traverse from Jason, to my hands clenched onto pathetic clumps of grass, and back before I suck air, grab his hand, and leap across.

I'm silent for the remainder of the hike up to the peak, my heart pounding from more than the exertion. I'm obsessing over having to go over that traverse again on the way back.

I chime in, "Think I'll take the back side down. Anybody want to go down that way with me? You know, it'd be nice to go another way and get a different view. Yes, I know it's another mile and a half extra walk back that way. Don't worry, I don't mind going by myself. Seriously you guys...don't feel like you have to come."

Still, I'm relieved when they say they'd like to go that way too.

Later that afternoon, a memory arose. Not a flash of the experience itself, but I recall a story that my mother had told me. She said when I was about two, not long after my father had left us, I'd toddled my way from the kitchen to the entranceway to a long set of cement stairs that led to the basement. She'd looked over to find me teetering there at the top before I went crashing all the way to the bottom. My mother's chair raked across the wooden floor as she rushed behind, she was sure I'd be dead.

I have no recollection of the fall, but it made me wonder if I had an unconscious memory that was connected to the intensity of the reaction I had on the mountain. How much or our lives then, is run by these unconscious memories and conditionings, like some of the things Ron speaks about, that has us behaving in ways that can be completely incongruent with the rationale of our minds.

Beyond that, the story makes me wonder how much I'd already felt and understood as a toddler. I have so much experience in my past of self-abuse, could it be that even then I was already toying with death?

I don't remember my father leaving, but in my mind's eye, I watch him descend the stairs, a tailored shirt on a hanger slung over his shoulder, and a black duffel bag in his hands. He pauses to watch my brother and I playing on the living room floor. Surely things hadn't turned out the way he'd thought with my mother. This isn't the life he wants to lead. He slips out, leaving us with a woman who was never been shown love and nurturing from her own parents, so had none to offer us. Nor had he. Surely he had no idea how important he was to us. He leaves, without understanding that a father's love and presence is a substance that is as necessary as food and water to nourish the body, mind and soul of his children.

I yearned for his presence my entire life, or at least to feel him and know he was there. My mother told me that when I was born, I fit perfectly into his hands. It's as if some deep, unknown part of me always remembered the safety and comfort of that, and in his leaving, so went with him any sensibility I'd have to receive true love or nurturing.

As I grew older, lost and afraid without him, I sought connection and pleasure through addictions. With no meaning or identity of my own, I sought to be saved with the love of my father through every man. Each partner became my value and foundation.

Ron hears my story, encouraging me to feel everything. We're sitting on his bed, and as I finish, he stacks a small pile of pillows to demonstrate a method for releasing anger, pain and resentment.

"I'm going to show you two good ways to let out negative emotions.

They're good tools to take responsibility, own your feelings, and release whatever triggers might be happening in the moment. This way, you can express your feelings without disturbing anyone else who might be around."

"First, you can do what I call a 'hand-scream,' like this!"

Ron takes a deep breath, cups his hands over his mouth, and screams into them while twisting his body in short jerks side to side as he kneels on the bed. His face grows bright red in the intensity of his release as he demonstrates, then he lets his hands go and turns back to pink.

"Ok, so the second method is pillow punching. You want to keep your spine straight while you bring your body forward, and hit the pillows with your forearms, like this." He leans down, performing a slow motion hit to the pillows, then shows me how I can plant my face into the pillows and scream as well.

"Ok, so let's try! Hay. Hay. Hay."

He starts chanting and breathing and directs me to do the same:

"Blink your eyes fast, and turn your head side to side, like this. Hay. Hay. Hay."

I feel ridiculous, but I had lived a traumatizing past, and I'm well aware of how pissed I can get in relationships. If I have resentment and anger, I definitely want to get rid of it.

I follow him, doing the breathing blinking thing for a few minutes, stop and take a deep breath and throw the my arms hard onto the pillow stack.

"HAH!" Nothing.

I try again, feeling for any sign of emotion,

"HAGH!" I punch the pillows hard, but start giggling and sit up again.

"I can see how this *will* be useful, but I'm not feeling much about it at the moment. I think I'm kind of over being mad at my dad anymore. I mean, I went through a whole life of grief around him already."

I pause.

"Wait, am I supposed to feel something?" My eyes roam side to side.

"I mean, I think there are places that I still do carry a lot of emotion, I guess kind of indirectly from my father's abandonment. Will it help if I share that?"

"Go for it!" Ron returns.

My shoulders drop and I look out the window at bare white branches.

"OK, so I think when I ran away, the main things I needed were basically love and attention. I needed a place to stay too, but as weird as it might sound, I think that felt secondary."

"Initially, I dealt with that by moving right in with older men. I'd already figured out that sex was what men wanted, and I wasn't in love with any of them. I wouldn't have admitted it at the time, in fact I don't think I've even really realized it until saying it now, but I think what I was doing was offering my body in trade. Sex and seduction were certainly my only sense of value and self worth. They were definitely what I relied on. Anyway, that's when I began to drink every weekend until I blacked out. I started waking up soaked in my own urine."

"I was always living in somebody else's home, and seeing that the convenient stores and gas stations didn't pay enough to live on my own, I was all too aware that if things went wrong, I'd be the one to go. I was scared, and with no safety or foundation, I was always on guard and reactive. Disagreements could never remain the simple truth of what they were. I still have this problem, in fact. When issues arise, it is never just the relationship that might be in question...but the basics: food, bed and a roof over my head are all threatened, and, of course, all of that is fed by my overall feeling of not being safe or loved. My world was an endless drama. I was needy and desperate, hopping place-to-place and man-to-man. Only after I began to sober, after twenty seven, could I even think to begin easing up on that pattern."

I sit in front of Ron, my eyes darting. I've rambled on and on, and haven't beaten a single pillow. Nevertheless, I haven't shared all of this with anyone and the permission to be open and vulnerable with someone who's inviting of it all is an enormous weight lifted from my shoulders. Ron lays me down, kisses my face and tells me I'm a beautiful Goddess, reminding me of his love. He offers sacred spot and we make love for hours and rest until the morning comes, and as I wake safe in his strong arms, my love for him begins to flood in.

It's just then that one of the first of Ron's lovers comes to the Temple for a visit.

Kristy's pretty and petite: busty with curly brown hair, doe eyes, and baby doll lips.

But I'm well prepared for this. Ron and I have already spoken about her and a few of his other lovers. He has assured me that Kristy is no threat to our relationship.

That day, Kristy and I took time alone together, hiking along the red trails behind the Temple, becoming accustomed to one another. Right off I like her, trusting in her intentions, and after the sun fell that night, I kissed Ron and Kristy both on the cheek as they cuddled into Ron's bed, and left them to go to my own room.

I've surprised myself. I'm not afraid or jealous in the least. I can do this.

In fact, since my arrival and over the last few weeks, Ron and I have been practicing Sacred Spot and making love several times a day, 'cultivating sexuality' as Ron calls it, as the main aspect of my training to become a Tantric Sexual healer.

In fact, Kristy being here is a bit of a relief. I'm quite happy to take a break from all the processing and sex. I sink under the covers, content and smiling, and relax into a deep sleep.

Chapter 18 ~ Questions of Sexual Freedom

Ron asks, "Are you up for talking a few minutes? Would you come outside to the fountains with me?" Ron pulls the blinds and they fold, one by one, into each other as the room floods with morning light. He slides open the glass doors and we step out onto the stone veranda, our breath condensing into the cool, winter air, while the stones underfoot are already warmed from the sun. Water dribbles from the top of the six-foot, stained glass mosaic lingam. Ron busies himself opening water filters to check for pine needles and leaves.

He tells me he'd like to create clarity and definition around our relationship, reminding me how wonderful it will be to travel the world, offering talks and workshops together.

"This work requires openness and vulnerability in order to create the deepest emotional healing. The attendees will feel safer with you by my side. I think there's some real potential for our success in together," he says, "We'll have plenty of private sessions along the way to keep us in abundance and spreading the love!"

Really, I want to solidify things as well. I'm becoming known as a Goddess: a Tantric Sacred Sexual Healer. I've become someone who is seen and appreciated, and life finally has more meaning. Beyond that, this is more luxury than I've ever known in the spaciousness of this beautiful temple home. The only thing that stands in the way of everything being completely perfect are my questions about Ron's sexual conduct:

There are the lovers, and as more time passes, their numbers, or at least my awareness of such, has risen exponentially.

As Dakinis and female friends come through the Temple, one by one, I come to find out the vast majority of them, if they are not presently lovers, have been at one time or another. It's rather uncanny.

Still, this is a relative and subjective preference, and as a polyamorist, he's free to make his sexual choices. But I have to admit, as the numbers grow, the more I feel disgusted with him.

But I'm learning, this is where I need to 'bring it home', relate these emotional triggers of the present to my past experience. In that context, it is true that my past was full of partners, one after the next, and I certainly felt shame around that.

Ron claims that his sexuality is healthy. Is that true? Am I holding judgment due to my own projections?

But more immediate questions loom over me, much greater than my personal concerns in relationship, if that be something that can truly be separated and distinguished; in this case it is proving itself a challenging emotional necessity:

I grow ever more weary and confused around the nature of Ron's sexual integrity with his work.

Through my own experience, I'm well aware that catharsis is fertile ground. His work as a Daka, a male sexual healer, is to walk his clients through their pain and wounds. A sexually traumatized woman that works with a Daka may become extremely emotionally open and vulnerable. He might even be her first encounter with a man where she feels safe and cared for. She then naturally feels deep love and appreciation, given the gift of a recipient to whom she can open her heart, and in those moments she raises him to a kind of emotional or Spiritual savior, and so also in those moments, her ability to make reasonable and healthy decisions around sex becomes easily skewed. It's a state that necessitates healthy integrity for a man in Ron's position: to professionally understand his responsibility in such a vulnerable position with a woman, and accordingly hold strong discernment and sexual boundaries.

But accusations of Ron's lack of integrity have continually arisen from past lovers, other Tantrics, and within talks and workshops, sometimes to the point of downright argument. Ron persistently points out that accusations directed at him are due to other's projections of shame, fear and guilt around sex, and I have to admit, there's been many times that I've observed for myself where he's spot on about that.

At the same time, I've often agreed with the truth of the accusations presented.

It's baffling: is this truly healing work, or is he fulfilling his own gratifications by taking advantage of the trust and vulnerability of his clients? When I've confronted him on this, he's responded, "Well, why should I not absolutely *love* my work?"

He speaks about the wounded vs. healthy masculine and feminine, healing childhood trauma and conditioned repression and obsession around sex.

Most everything he says sounds wonderful and ideal, but his words just don't seem to match his actions. What I feel I'm experiencing is a perpetual, one-way rocket of a man obsessed with sex. He wants sex with me several times a day, and if it's not with me, he's with other lovers or clients. If he's not actually having sex, he's masturbating, and if not that, on some level or the other, he's talking about sex!

Sex!

Sex!

Sex!

On the other hand, he's been a Tantric Sexual healer for twenty years. I don't know anything about sexual healing. I've been here a few months. I have to consider that this confusion and anguish may very well be the natural process of healing my wounds and conditionings around sex, of course I'd hold such judgments.

Certainly I've watched plenty of women leave the Temple after sessions with Ron looking renewed, happy and grateful. I love to see the places he supports people. In so many cases, he does it so well.

I don't, I cannot decipher here between the light and the shadow.

I'd say this might not be the best conditions for a partnership.

"Ron, I really enjoy our time together, and I'm excited to learn all I can." I lean down and help him pull leaves from the pond, "but I have to be honest. I really don't think I'm in love in the way that's right for a partnership."

Ron turns away from me while I finish speaking, attending to a nearby fountain. "Well...that's good," he says.

It is? I watch him, puzzled.

"I need someone like you as a partner."

He pulls a fistful of wet leaves from the cold fountain waters.

"With my lifestyle, I really don't need someone who'll be so attached." He turns and sits, inviting me next to him.

"We'll begin with the next three months, check in and see if we want to continue in this partnership." I nod, my eyes darting through the yard.

"Are you with me?" David asks, his soft brown eyes searching mine. "Remember what you most love about Ron."

I look above David's shoulder. Kala, David's partner, is now climbing on top of Ron, passionately kissing him. Less than an hour ago, she'd been a stranger. All I know about her is she's an ex-prostitute with a tough demeanor and fake breasts. I haven't exactly warmed up to her yet.

David, on the other hand, is the first Daka I have met that I've really, intuitively, trusted. He's kind hearted and beautiful with curly black locks, long lashes and thick lips... and he dresses all Saddhu in malas and flowing white Indian cotton. He'd made quite an impression the first night we'd met.

We were in the hot tub, he and myself and Ron, when my mouth, hands and feet suddenly began to tingle. The sensation grew, and in a matter of minutes, I had lost all muscular control and my fingers and wrists were curling in on themselves. I was frightened and Ron wrapped me in a towel and brought me to my bed.

"It's energy moving where it's unaccustomed," Ron said. "It's natural. People often get it in breathing practices. Just relax, concentrate on your breath, and it'll go away soon."

It took a while, but the sensation did eventually dissipate, and I was totally renewed. I realized then how intensely I was affected just by standing in a pool of water with David. I'd been in that tub plenty of times with Ron, but I'd never experienced any kind of reaction like that.

So... what's David doing with this bitch?

"I thought he'd talk with me about this first!" I whisper, loudly enough that I hope Ron overhears as I fight a wave of tears. I don't trust this. Just before we came into the bedroom, I came upon Kala and Ron by the hearth. She was sitting astride him, masturbating him, while he lay naked on a sarong. I watched, not knowing what else to do, while she pulled, rubbed, twisted, slapped, and shook his cock with astounding vigor and technique.

"Breath with me." David tries to pull me back.

My head spins. Isn't a partnership about making decisions together?

Doing things at a pace that works for both of us?

Doesn't he know I'm right here feeling this? Isn't he paying attention? Hasn't he heard me when I've said it's too much? He moves so damn fast!

I mean, David's wonderful, I feel him, I trust him, but still, I don't need to fuck him.

I'm in over my head. This isn't at all the picture I had of polyamory or Sacred sex. But then again, I am here to learn to be a Dakini and heal my sexual dysfunctions, and as Ron says, it's my shame and guilt and fear that holds me back from being the Goddess, being limitless unconditional Love, and my opportunity to learn is right here, straddling the man I'd like to surrender with.

The problem is I just can't seem to do that because he's always fucking another woman!

I take a deep breath, and lay my head down, trying to remain present with David.

"Share with me what you most love about him."

Moans arise next to us. Absolutely. Fucking. Nothing.

I need to surrender. Concentrate. Breathe.

Ron and Kala's heightened breath, the smack of wet lips and twirling tongues bores through me from the other side of the bed. I don't know how far they will go. All I do know is what Ron has made clear: his sexuality is his, and he will go into "Sacred Union" with a woman if that is his desire and it is for "the highest good."

What does that mean? Is that really only up to his discernment? Is this feeling the highest good? I bury my face into David's chest. This feels more like the road to hell than to Spiritual sex and love.

I'm alone with my arms folded over the side of the hot pool, warming the anguish and autumn chill from my bones. Fairy chimes play in cool winds that sweep through my hair. I hear the sound of Ron wading into the water behind me.

He comes over and kisses my shoulder and my cheek and wraps his arms around me from behind.

"Hello my sweet beloved," he whispers into my ear. I bury my face in my arms.

"Come here." he says, and turns me around to face him.

My brows push toward each other when I look into his eyes. He lifts one of my legs, then the other, and wraps me around his waist. I sigh and rest my head onto his shoulder to surrender into his embrace as he wades me through the warm water, like a father might hold a hurting child. Tears run down my cheeks and stream over his shoulders.

"You're my beloved," he says. "None of my other lovers will ever threaten our partnership."

I want to believe it.

The following morning, thoughts turn over and over in my mind. Why am I so threatened by Ron's pace and level of sexuality? I came here for the very purpose of learning freedom, to cast off my conditionings around relationship and sex. Yet Ron's sexual behavior disgusts me, why?

Where is it that I've experienced conditioning or trauma around sexual freedom?

Then, a memory arises, somewhere just out of high school:

Fred and I were just getting to know each other, so we weren't clearly defined or committed, but I had a serious crush on him. He was tall, athletic, gorgeous, and confident, and hung out with the rich kids and the jocks. He requested I attend a party with him, and it was there that I'd experience Fred's method of investigating into my sexual inclinations.

As usual, I drank myself into a fog and was blinking through the chaos of conversation. Fred took my hand and led me through a brightly lit kitchen, I staggering and squinting behind, until we made it to a gently lit bedroom. Automatically, I crawl into the bed in drunken reprieve from the bustle of the party. Fred undressed me, and images of our lovemaking arose and fell into darkness, and Fred was above me when a quiet sliver of light entered the room, grew larger, and his friend Randy crept in. Randy comes over and sits on the corner of the bed. Fred, still inside of me, greets him and whispers into my ear.

"Would you like to make love with Randy as well? He'd love it, and I wouldn't mind at all," he says.

It took me all aback.

"Really?" I say.

I'd never considered sharing like that, but Randy's gorgeous and Fred's inviting this, and it all looks quite appetizing at the moment.

"Yes, ok. Really, it wouldn't upset you?" I ask.

"No, I'd like it." He responds, and pulls out of me and begins to get up. It's all a bit weird and sudden. I was thinking he'd stay, but he gets up to dress while Randy climbs in. I'm not sure about this but Randy's climbing over me. Fred puts his hands on his hips, smiles and wishes us a fun time, and leaves the room, shutting the door quietly behind him.

Sex with Randy's a bizarre non-event. He was soft and entered me anyway right away, and only momentarily, then backed out, and whispered that he'd always wanted to make love to me. I lay in dumb silence, confused with the disparity between his words and the momentary encounter. Randy ups himself, dressed, thanked me, and stepped out of the room. I lay there alone in the dark, uncomfortable and suddenly sober, realizing the party might have caught wind of what just occurred. My heart begins to pound. I slide out of bed and quickly dress, only to sit on the bed in the dark gnawing my nails before venturing out to find Fred.

I crack open the door into the blaring light and step out, squinting in vain attempt to find the safety of Fred's open arms. I stepped out and as I meandered through the kitchen, unmistakable expressions of disgust stared me down. I began to shake automatically, suddenly alone in a hostile group of strangers. I couldn't find Fred, but I did spot Randy. Relieved, I walk towards him. He turns and sees me approaching, and without expression, looks away.

I stop in my tracks.

Of that night, I have no further recollection.

Chapter 19 ~ Running with Dinosaurs

R on taps on my bedroom door and pops his head inside.

"Hi, honey," he says with a loving smile. He's carrying a fresh bouquet of sunflowers to replace the roses he brought last week that are slowly wilting... much like I am. Last night, Ron and I argued about intercourse with clients. It's a topic on which we simply can't reach agreement.

"As long as my belly, my body and my mind are all in alignment, and it's all for the highest good, then yes, a client can pay for sex," is his typical position statement.

I'll grant that such words have some validity if spoken by the right persons. But each individual is a collage of a billion various shades of initiatives, drives, perceptions, and projections. How does one determine who's truly capable of such wisdom and discernment?

Of course, Ron's response is accurate enough in the context of prostitution. Two consenting adults equipped with floggers, butt plugs, dildos, hog tied naked from ceiling fans, singing "Lucy in the Sky With Diamonds," with thousand dollar bills taped to every toe is just fine if that is what they wish. But I have serious issues with discernment when it comes to this work being advertised as a healing practice.

Sex has a lot to do with power, as the BDSM folks are quick to point out. And in his position—my position as well now, apparently—he has to be fully aware of the awesome responsibility within the context of this work.

It seems to me that only the wisest and most discerning of souls would be developed enough: not only to ignore their own desires, but also to have done enough work on themselves to not even be possessed of such an array of desires. Why does he need so many fulfillments from others? Are they truly acting for their clients' highest good? Dakas should know how women in our society are deeply conditioned to think their value is contingent upon their relationships with men, their outer appearance, seductiveness and sexuality. But even the bulk of Tantrikas are all about seduction, playing right into the same game. I mean, it seems to me that being run by desires, and dependence on sex and seduction, are some of the things Dakas and Dakinis should be focused on healing. There is so much messy energy around this Tantric scene!

I pull my mind back to focus.

Isn't monetary exchange for sex appropriate only after working with someone over a period of time, attentive to her progress, all done with the greatest care and discernment?

Ron is in a powerful position of authority. I know from my own experience that women are at risk of giving away their power and offering themselves sexually to a man when they feel a lack of power and authority within themselves. Shouldn't that be the job of a true Daka: to help a woman learn how to stand confidently and make more appropriate decisions about her body and sex, rather than giving away her power and falling into culturally enforced roles and values?

What if Ron's fast track sexuality is reinforcing the same old constructs?

Ron tilts his head and arranges the flowers perfectly in their vase. It's a ritual he never forgets, and however upset I might be, it melts me every time.

He comes over and sits on the bed and pulls me into his arms.

"Today I have a session with a very sweet couple. I've worked with them before. The wife, her name's Karen, has specifically requested for you to be there."

I release myself from his arms.

"Ron, I can't do a session. How? I don't know what I'm doing!"

"You know what you're doing more than you think." Ron says. "Laurel, You are a very powerful woman and Dakini. It's who you are. Your presence is enough." He kisses me on my cheek. "Trust and witness, and be with whatever comes." He says, and lifts my arms to remove my shirt.

"Let's make love," he says. "We'll say a prayer and call in the energies we need. They'll be here in three hours. We'll be ready for them."

Fortunately, I don't have any time to be nervous. We make love and jump into the shower and dress and just as we finish, Ron's clients are at the door for their session.

Karen's a thin woman with medium length, light brown hair and amber eyes, and her husband Rico is dark with a thick accent: I'm guessing Iranian. She was abused early on by a babysitter and has never had an orgasm. It's clear where we're headed: it seems the plan was already made as she's mostly addressing me towards the issue at hand.

Karen's nervous and timid, but she's determined to work through this. We all undress so everyone in the room is naked and vulnerable on the bed; she's not alone. I sit behind her so she can rest her head in my lap, while Ron sits between her legs and her husband holds her hand at her side. We all comfort her and give her time to relax as Ron massages her legs and thighs. Ron guides her through the emotions of her past trauma, and I stroke her forehead and wipe her tears as she cries, and watch as her fear and pain transforms to pleasure. When her massage is complete, she looks up, beautiful and teary eyed, and thanks me while we hold hands and I run my fingers through her hair. She tells me she's so grateful to have the opportunity to work through this safely. We'd all fallen in love, our client's eyes beaming as they left the temple.

Several hours later, I'm walking back to his room, ready to share with him how much my heart is singing. We'd spoken after our session about Sex Magic, a practice he introduced to me that he'd like to bring into our practice. Sexual energy, he explained, is the most powerful energy humans have, and it can be used to manifest all that we desire by harnessing the intensity of orgasmic energy. He told me that with this magic, we could say our prayer to clean and purify rivers and lakes and forests.

I'm ready to love and trust him deeper, ready to practice Sex Magic and support the planet. But when I find Ron, he's in front of his bedroom door speaking with a woman. He tells me he's just about to go in with a client. I've seen her before.

I wonder if this is one that pays for sex. I turn around and go back to the living room. Breathe, I remind myself as I wrap into a blanket and throw myself into a pillow in front of the hearth.

Carlos Castaneda had eaten Datura, and was tumbling around with dogs on the floor, when Ron and his client showed up into the living room after the completion of their session. I peek above my book, watching Ron and his client embrace before she disappears out the door. Setting my book on the table, I lift myself from the warmth of my blanket, take my tea and stand by the back doors to watch the view of majestic red hills stand against stark blue New Mexican skies.

I feel Ron approaching from behind before he wraps his arms around me and I snuggle into his arms, rest my head back onto his shoulder, and take his hands into mine.

They feel clammy.

I lift my head.

Suddenly I smell it, the sex of that woman still on him.

I whip my head around, shove his hands away and glare at him.

"That's enough! Wash your fucking hands after a session! I don't want someone else's juices on me, Okay! Come on! It's common sense, Ron!"

"Honey," his eyebrows apex as he shakes his head, "Sex and juices are sacred!"

His words, 'sex and juices', seem to drool from his mouth.

My jaw clenches. I hold my tongue as I rinse my mug in the sink, set it in the drain and storm out.

My head spins:

I throw myself onto my bed, grab a pillow, smash my face into and scream and kick my legs. *He's a fucking prostitute! I didn't want a prostitute as a partner!*

I hit the pillow- hard- and scream into it again.

WHY DO YOU HAVE TO FUCK EVERYTHING THAT MOVES! FUCK!

I slam the pillow over and over again, until I want something more satisfying and hold my fist taught, aimed at the wall.

And pause. *You don't want to hurt yourself. Come on.*

Okay, breathe. Why does this bother me so much? Is this about him or me?

Can't prostitution at the same time be healing work? What's the difference? Isn't sex beautiful? Seriously, why does this all bother me so much?

I can't decipher the appropriate lines. It's all become so grey.

This is the situation I came into. I know I need to take my feelings around our personal relationship and try to separate that from his healing work.

I really have to do better than this. I've become a human yo-yo.

One moment I'm proud by his side, inspired by his ideals, impressed with his wit. He's completely 'on' as a teacher, supporting people to own their power and come to terms with their sexual wounds. The next, he's the sexually wounded one, playing the role of teacher so he can save the world, projecting it all outside of himself. On another day, his eyes somehow grow small and his very smell is repulsive. He's a sexual manipulator, seeking pleasure because he cannot bear the pain and desperation that lives inside of him: pleasure from totally inappropriate places: from clients, new lovers every week... I'm sure something's off about all this.

And so many teachers come through here, every one of them older, wiser, and certainly more experienced than I. Everyone talks about it, but no one is standing up. Why? I want to slam my head against the wall.

I call Mark. He was moving out of the temple months ago, just as I was moving in. He'd lived there for a good year and a half previous. Mark strikes me as someone with integrity, so I invite him to breakfast. Surely he's seen it all, and I'm sorely in need of perspective.

In response to my prattling on about all of my confusions, Mark looks at me deadpan:

'Basically you're in relationship with a sex addict,' he says.

I sit there blinking at him while King Kong steps down from my shoulders.

'But sometimes you've just got to run with the dinosaurs.'

Mark's the first person who's been honest with me about this. Ron's mentors haven't. His friends haven't. People I respect haven't.

Thank god, I'm not just nuts. Or, am I, because with said addiction confirmed, I'd normally just wipe my hands clean of this, but there's the second part of his statement. I meet Mark's stolid grey eyes.

"What do you mean...you just got to run with dinosaurs?"

"Stick with it, Laurel. You're a skimmer." I raise a brow. "You jump from one thing to the next."

How does he know that?

"You're here. Stay long enough to really get the lessons from this experience." Mark goes to work buttering a croissant. I don't know whether to feel pained or inspired.

Of course, the day arrives when I can't hold back, and I use Mark's words as a weapon in the throes of my discouragement:

"This has to stop!" I stand in front of Ron with my hands on my hips, pacing in front of him while he peels bananas and spoons spirulina into a blender, making smoothies for us. Another lover just walked out the door.

"I know you have a sex addiction, Ron!" The big guns: "Even Mark's confirmed it!"

I stop and glare at him.

"Honey, come on." Ron shakes his head and chuckles.

"I don't have an addiction. You know who I am."

Ron shrugs and smiles at me real big. "I just love to love!"

I throw my hands in the air. "Sex isn't the only thing to love!" I howl.

"Honey, Mark said that because he's gay." Ron tells me. "Since I wouldn't sleep with him, he moved out and started spreading rumors that I have a sex addiction."

My lids drop to half-mast: *of course.*

I watch Ron, shirtless and muscular in his sarong while he runs the blender and pours thick green liquid into two long glasses and hands one to me, still grinning. I take the drink, staring at him, and turn to stalk out of the room.

Chapter 20 ~ Becoming a Tantric Sexual Healer

I'm sitting on a pillow in the living room, staring into my computer screen. Brenda's listed my picture on the temple site: "Goddess Laurel, available for sessions," along with a headshot Ron had taken the first day I walked into the Temple. I look way too young and naive to be a so-called Goddess. I'm not even close to being ready for this.

The front door opens and Daka Chris struts into the temple. He's thin and muscular with tribal tattoos across the width of his back, sky blue eyes and blonde locks that fall over his shoulders. I have a crush on him, but I also have a strong connection with his lover, Aya. He's poly, but her trust is a greater priority than my curiosities. Regardless of his push and assurances of the openness of their relationship, it's a line I don't need to cross without her absolute blessing and consent.

Perhaps it's the very solidity of the ground I stand on around this that makes him so intent on moving the goal posts around.

He kneels down next to me, shining his blues into mine; "HellOooo," he says with his thick German accent. I wrap my arm around him and push my computer screen into his view. "Look." I say flatly. "They've got me on the site already."

"Hmmmnnn." Chris moans. His eyes snake from the computer back to me and he raises and drops his brows several times.

"Book me in for a session." I push his hand off my knee.

"Seriously. I'm not ready for sessions." I say.

"You can practice on me," he says with a devilish grin, placing a hand over his chest. "I'm more than willing to sacrifice my time to support the cause."

I groan, jump up, and pace the room.

"Chris, I'm serious. I don't have any real training. How am I gonna do this? People study for all their lives to be teachers and Shamans... but it's fine, I just mosey in and start healing people. That makes sense!

I don't even have experience giving *normal* massage, how, am I supposed to give a sensual one? And at two hundred dollars an hour! Shit, at that rate, it *better* feel good!" I'm pacing, waving my arms around.

Chris leans back on the pillow, interlacing his fingers behind his neck, and his eyes follow me with the corners of his lips curled up.

He tells me all I have to do is what comes natural.

"Laurel, you're ready. You just have to start."

I kneel down in front of him and look deadpan into his eyes.

"Seriously, you're telling me that's what you did? You had no real training. You knew nothing. You just started."

"I must have known something. Just like you do." Chris grins, stretches out his arms, and gazes around the room.

"School of Life!"

I plop down onto the pillow on the floor and scrunch my face into my palms.

Brenda walks over from the office and calls my name. I pull my face from my hands. She hands me a yellow sticky note and kneels down next to me, and with her finger, underlines the script she'd written upon it:

Ben Martin 857-928-4228.

"This gentleman just called in response to your ad on the site. He's been here before, so he's a legit client. Can you give him a call? I told him you'd get a hold of him by tomorrow afternoon. He's coming... I think he said the eighteenth of next month. He's excited to meet you."

I double take.

"Brenda, I can't take this yet. I'm..."

Brenda pops up. Her phone's ringing and she heads back to the office. "By tomorrow, ok?" She flashes me a smile over her shoulder and runs to the phone. I look at the date on my computer.

Three weeks. Three weeks before my first session!

I close my computer.

"I could cry."

Daka Chris, giggling, heads over to speak with Brenda.

"I'm here if you need the practice," he says, spreading his arms, walking backwards.

I roll my eyes.

So I watch videos, listen to audios and practice the Tantric Orbit. I sun-gaze, eye-gaze, and walk slow and barefoot. I research Kundalini, the seven Chakras and their Sanskrit names, their qualities, placements, and colors. I pore over books on Astrology, Shamanism, and past life regression.

I get five enemas in a row and give myself a liver-cleanse.

And I accept Chris' offer for practice, as well as others, and have lots and lots of sex with Ron.

And in the turn on and pace and intention of it all, I decide to move forward, to completely step into my work as a Sacred Sexual practitioner.

There are two websites that advertise Tantrics. One of them is condensed alongside prostitution ads with a section for Tantra listings. You click onto flashing images of breasts, women on their hands and knees shot from behind, arching in bliss with legs spread wide. The other site, although solely based on Tantra, is nevertheless much of the same: seductive images with write-ups that speak of Tantra's healing qualities, each one of them dripping with terms like, 'juicy' 'Sacred' and 'orgasmic bliss'. Two women hold each other naked, lips parted: 'Double Goddess Sessions' it says. I squeeze my temples. I don't pretend to know a thing about Tantra, but it doesn't take a rocket scientist to realize this has nothing to do with India's ancient practices.

Where, I'm wondering, is the Sacred in all of this?

I call Jenna in Austin, a friend of Ron's who had initially helped me to make the decision to come to the Temple. She seemed a lot more grounded than some of the women I'd thus far become acquainted in this work.

"What's up with the Tantric Ads? Are there really no other choices?"

"Nope." she says "That's it."

"I don't understand." I say, "Where does actual Tantra fit into this? I mean, I get there can be major healing in sessions, I've experienced that, but from what I can see, there's initiatives and intentions all over the map. I mean, where's the line between the Sacred and the profane?"

Jenna giggles.

"Think of it as the carrot. You're meeting your clients where they're at. Then, when they come, you show them something deeper, something more real."

I go silent, taking in her words, and sigh.

"Jenna, I don't know about all of this."

"You know, the only thing that will show you the truth- your own truth- is your experience. Looks like it'll be soon, too. I saw they got you up on the site!"

"Jeez! Stuff moves fast in these circles!" I say, "but Laurel and all of her past; that girl's got to go. Anyway, I'm not comfortable with the idea of my legal name in those ads."

"Have you a new one yet?"

"I think so." I say.

"This whole thing's pretty surreal, and I want to keep reminder of the intention that brought me here: to see through fears and conditionings around sex and relationship.

So what do you think of Maya? I've actually always coveted that name, and in Hindu religion, Maya refers to the *illusion*."

"I like it!" Jenna says.

That evening I light a candle and hold over the flame a slip of paper on which I'd written my name along with a list of undesirable thoughts and patterns, and watch it all burn to ash. The following morning, I placed an ad on the Tantric Temple website under a new name: 'Goddess Maya.'

I'm still feeling the Goddess thing's a bit pretentious, but the site automatically categorizes you as such, so here I am, a seductive Goddess, wading right into the shallow... objectifying the very sexuality that I came to the Temple to move away from. Still, at least in my write-up, I try to portray the healing intention of my sessions. But as I look the ad over, insecurity rushes in. I want to be a sexual healer, but what does that really mean? If I'm not offering sex, who's going to call, and what, exactly, *am* I offering? Ron has continually assured me that I don't have to, nor should I, do anything I don't want to do. I just have to be authentic, be myself, and be natural. I don't have to be sexual at all.

I begin taking calls:

"Do you offer oral stimulation? Sacred Spot Massage? Goddess Worship? Sacred Union? BDSM? Domination? Submission? Can I dress as a woman? Wear nylons? Handcuffs? Will you be naked? Will I? Can I touch? How much IS appropriate, then?"

"Do you offer...release?" My caller asks.

"Well ...um, emotion release, yes, but if you're strictly looking for sensual massage, you might be better off looking elsewhere. I don't offer that on the first session."

"How about on the second?"

"Well, I can't guarantee anything. It all depends on if it's appropriate."

"What would be required to make it appropriate?"

"You'd find that out in session." *I have no idea.*

"Do you offer massage at all?"

"Well, I'm not professionally trained, but of course I'll offer loving touch if it's feeling right to do so."

"Is it pleasurable?"

"Um," I tap my thumb with the end of my pen "I...haven't had any complaints." My intonation rises while I squeeze the bridge of my nose.

"Anyway, if you want sensual massage, I can direct you to someone else who will. Otherwise, would you still like to book a session?"

"What is it I do in my sessions? Oh, um ... I offer clarity."

Somehow it all comes together, and for the first two weeks I manage to skirt sensual massage altogether and, to my surprise, a handful of men still book sessions. As for the rest, the Dakinis visiting the temple as of late love me for all the referrals I'm sending their way. And as sessions begin, I'm discovering profound things can happen with two people in a room with a sincere healing intention:

Richard sits across from me: a soft and gentle middle-aged man with sky blue eyes, thin lips and rosy Santa Clause cheeks. He's got a piece of paper with poetry he's written on his lap. He'd like to begin the session by reading a poem to help me become acquainted with him. He stands up straight, clears his throat and waggles his head.

'Love's Reign'

Searching for a land where love may reign.
Securing salvation for the soul to reclaim.

Inheriting hollow answers over the years.

Sorrow drops a spirit in the form of tears,
Drenched with sadness in a drowning rain,
Our Souls Seek love, echoing a hearts refrain.

Hoping for freedom from fear and shame,
Searching for a land where love may reign.

In fear and shame, a soul screams out,
A primal query, as it wanders about,
For whom, why, and what on earth for?
Madness born from false religious fervor.

Clinging to our minds, our sanity to maintain,
Onward we walk to where love might reign.

In anguish, the human heart earnestly asks,
Exhausted in searching beyond outward reach,
It prays for the truth, and unveiling our masks,
Looking inward, a begging soul does beseech,
To discover its own truth, in performing its task,
Yielding joyful sounds, replacing normal speech.

Created to love fully and freely, our heavenly design,
Recognizing our unity, reflecting all as divine.
In experiencing our true nature, we now maintain,

Birthright of a loving world, our inherited domain.

The soul is eternally free to sing loving refrains,
Being divine truth, understanding love always reigns.

Richard looks up and places his hand on his heart.

"I just had to share some of myself with you, Maya. I'm on this healing journey and I truly hope we can share our deepest selves with each other."

I take in the tenderness of the man who's come into my space, invite him to rest on the bed, and ask him if he feels safe to walk me through a childhood memory.

"I'd be willing, as long as you'll stay with me. "

I ask him to imagine himself as a little boy and he closes his eyes and the room grows quiet and still:

He's wearing a green and yellow striped shirt, jean shorts and socks. Sky blue eyes look up at me, and a tiny hand reaches up to take mine. He walks me through his house: the den, a long hallway with family photos all along the walls between a large wooden cross and images of Christ and Mary, blue robed and in prayer. He takes me up a long stairwell towards his room and suddenly squeezes my hand as he stops in his tracks. "He's coming!" Richard whispers.

I open my eyes to see Richard as a man- his belly rising and falling at a faster pace, tiny moans escaping him as he turns his head side to side.

"No."

I close my eyes again.

Richard's father glares at him from the bottom of the stairs and slowly begins to climb. Richard lets go of my hand and runs ahead. His father rushes after, on his tail into Richard's room. I follow them: a desk, white dresser with a radio and a bed with a blue comforter. Richard is scrambling to squeeze himself beneath the bed in a desperate attempt to hide. I open my eyes again; tears stream down Richard's cheeks. He moans and his body writhes and squirms as his father grabs him by the ankle to drag him out. He slides across the floor, struggling to flip over and as he does, he sees the leather of his father's belt and holds his arms up to protect his face as his father lashes upon him. Richard curls up on the bed moaning and crying and I tell him I'm going to protect him. I tell him I'm pulling his father away and am placing him in a special force field that he can't escape from. Richard's body relaxes and begins to quiet. I ask him if he'd like to be held and he nods in approval.

After some time, when Richard's completely calm, I stroke the top of his head and ask if he'd be willing to discourse with his father. Lifting my chin towards the corner of the room, I tell Richard: "He's still locked in the force field over there. You're completely safe. If I let him out, I can put him back in whenever I want. Your father told me he'd like to talk with you. How would you feel about that? Would you be willing to exchange a few words with him?"

In real life, his dad has already passed away, and Richard's never had the chance to tell him how painful things were for him as a child. Richard looks to the corner of the room pensively and than back to me.

"Oh Maya," he says, shaking his head with his lips pressed together. "I think that would be a good idea, for him and for me. Okay. Yeah. Let's do that."

Richard shifts in his seat and sits up tall.

I set down two pillows across from each other on the bed, and guide Richard first to sit on one.

"Remember. Just say the word and I'll put the force field back around him."

Richard closes his eyes and tells me his father looks calm and peaceful: more than he'd ever seen him. I ask if he'd be willing to tell his dad how he feels.

"Well." Richard forces out a sigh and opens his eyes a moment before settling back and pauses with his eyes closed again.

Richard speaks his piece, and then switches seats back and forth, speaking his position and then playing the role of his father in response. Towards the end of the discourse, his father goes silent, bows his head and places his hand on his heart. He apologizes, explaining to Richard what prompted his rage: his own abusive upbringing, insecurity and helplessness as a man during the stirrings of war, poverty, and, he knew it was wrong to drink, but he couldn't think clearly. He was so scared and overwhelmed. He didn't know what else to do.

I invite Richard to continue the dialogue, this time taking the seat of his own self again and this time, I take the role of his father.

"When you were born I held you in my hands. Your mother and I were so happy. You were so precious and tiny. If only I knew then what I do now. But so much happened. I only wish I could have expressed the love I felt for you. I was so messed up. I'm so sorry. I love and miss you so much, Richard." I say.

Richard holds a hand over his heart as tears stream from his eyes.

I lay him down, feeling safe to offer him some loving touch on the massage table.

He tells me he's had chronic sciatic pain since he was a child, and directs me to the areas where he fees pain. I run my hands over him, and indeed, heat and heaviness hovers around his body. Fascinated, I close my eyes and concentrate, and in my mind's eye, a sword and dark masses are lodged within him. I don't know if it's real or just imagination, but instinct says to pull them, and as I proceed, he reacts strongly as if he's feeling their removal. None of this makes sense. I don't even know the cause of sciatic pain. But anyway something's happening, so I go with it.

So begins my training, at least in playing the part of Tantric Sexual Healer. I don't understand it myself, but Richard would send me an email a month later, and then check in consecutive months to inform me that I had relieved him of life long sciatic pain. That had never happened to him before. Go figure.

Men come to my room and tell me stories of shadows that lurk throughout the backdrop of their lives, weaving webs that entangle the paths of each thought and action, or engulf so completely, they're worn as masks. The roles of student to teacher shifts and changes: we alternate masks, holding mirrors to reflect each other, or drop them altogether to stand before each other vulnerable and naked. We shine light on fears that blind and pain that paralyzes. Their stories pull me back in time to the cliff's edge and the valley of the shadow of death. I know these places well and can guide them through the terrain of the land. For the first time, I realize I've got a gift: a talent borne through the intensity of my life's experience.

I'm familiar with the stained-glass maze of addictions, obsessions and avoidance, the language of denial and lack of self-confidence, the overwhelming feelings of desperation and loneliness, the hopelessness of a life without meaning. Granted... I've made only the most fundamental of progressions.

The response of my clients is profound and none of it makes sense. Perhaps simply the healing power of prayer and intention is enough; that combined with sheer naïveté. Whatever the reason, I'm learning that I don't have to know what to do except get out of my own way. Clearly, I'm not rowing this boat alone.

Nevertheless, there's part of this role I've yet to face with someone I don't know. The more men share with me their feelings around sex, the shame, guilt and fear that hang over them, their stories of abuse and manipulation, and their concerns with performance and expectation, the more I can see how these men would indeed benefit from a compassionate and loving touch, without risk, or the strings of emotional attachment. So when a client came to me with the pain and anxiety of premature ejaculation, it was there that I began.

"I go into fantasies when I make love with a woman."

John's a tall, lanky man that swims in his beige, collared shirt, loose jeans and loafers. "I've had lovers, but for most of my life, it's been short affairs or one-nighters. I had a girlfriend for almost a year once, but that's about it. I think I've known for a good long while I've got issues with intimacy, but I've just kind of let it go, life just moves along."

I back the conversation, inquiring into his past. Small, sorrel eyes meet mine then fall to the rug. He lifts himself an inch from the armchairs and shifts in his seat.

"When I was a child," he says "if I was scared or cried or, I don't know, even if I just asked for what I wanted, my parents would tell me to buck up and take life like a man. They'd make me sit in the corner with nothing. Sometimes they locked me in the closet. I hated it. I think it was in that closet that I learned how to go into fantasyland. I don't think I've ever been in touch with my body or my feelings. When it comes to intimacy with a woman, I don't really know what to do. When a woman gets emotional, that's when I exit...so I always, eventually, exit."

I lay him down on the table on his belly to massage the muscles on his shoulders and back, knead his legs and arms, then turn him over to stroke and caress every part of him from fingers to toes. I'm noticing the need I'd felt for technical training in massage had all but melted. Who

John is, his intention is enough to invoke some part of me that simply desires to love and support him. My touch comes naturally.

As I massage the front of his body, I ask if he'd be comfortable if I was to sit between his legs and touch the entirety of his body. He responds positively, so I climb onto the table, straddling it, and rest his legs upon mine.

I caress his lingam, as part of him rather than the entire focus of attention, and ask him to breath deep, feeling his belly rise as it fills with air, and fall as he exhales. He's relaxing under my hands, able to let go of concern with pleasing, stamina, or the pressure of performance in conjunction with attention and touch to his genitals.

Our eyes and breath meet and I encourage him to maintain his breath, and then focus upon the silence available in his mind.

"Thoughts come as they do, like clouds passing through the blue sky. Try not to focus upon or chase the clouds: the passing thoughts." I say, "but rather allow them to arise and pass, maintaining your attention on the sky."

I cup my hands over his now erect lingam, massaging slow and gentle, supporting him to communicate with me so we can monitor his level of excitement.

"Where are you on a scale from one to ten?" I ask.

His eyes shift right to left.

"About a seven, but that can rise really quick."

I slow my already gentle pace so that I'm barely moving and we remain there, only slightly shifting pace here and there with no goal. His eyes travel, and each time I remind him to return. For several minutes we remain quietly present together, and as he fully relaxes and stills himself, his erection begins to fade and his eyes begin to well and suddenly he begins to talk about my beauty. I thank him and gently request he simply focus inside, feel what's going on with his body, allow any feelings to arise. It was all the permission he needed. Tears pour down his face onto his naked chest and shoulders. Through his tears he tells me: at forty-five years of age, this is the first time in a sensual context he'd ever felt calm and safe. The remainder of the session, we lay sweetly embracing.

John left the Temple oozing gratitude and thanks, and I'm standing in the living room with several hundred dollars in my hand, more than I'd requested or expected. I curl my fingers over the bills and walk back down the hall, high with the sweetness and vulnerability of our session.

What was I so worried about?

I'd just given my first sensual massage, the very thing I'd feared and judged, and it was some of the most precious and gentle moments I'd ever experienced with a man.

I get to help people and love on them and bring them comfort and happiness.

I'm not even clear if this is fair: this is the best I've ever been paid and I think I'm receiving as much healing and benefit as my clients are.

It's dawning on me that I've landed in the best occupation in the world!

Each of the men that comes to me in search of growth and healing for their sexual wounds and distortions opens my heart and teaches me how to trust. My past had impressed upon me such an image of men as ethically weak, slaves to their desires, somehow estranged to the depths of love and wisdom. But these men are dissolving my old ideas, each one of them has, in their own unique way, been a friend and mentor.

Ironically, It's Ron, my partner, saving grace and the very life behind all of this, who is the one that reflects the shadowy and ego driven aspects: Sex obsession, manipulation... the wanting, needy, grasping man.

Yet he's been doing this for twenty years. It's his expertise. He's the teacher.

I wander the halls of my own private little mind fuck.

Chapter 21 ~ Tantric World Tour

This shift in experience, the radical pace of lifestyle is too much to clearly understand, let alone integrate: almost overnight I've become a Sacred Sexual practitioner on a Tantric world tour, followed around by a pair of producers Ron's hired:

He'd wanted to create a documentary on Tantra and his work, and inquired if I'd be keen on Mike and Johah, on occasion, filming the events of our lives together. I shrugged indifferent approval.

Sometimes they turn up out of nowhere; in the middle of dinner, a ripe cherry tomato explodes as I chew, sputters over my lip, and down my cleavage. I dig for juicy seeds, eating each one captured, and look up to find a camera catching the whole thing: terribly uncivilized for a so-called Dakini. Nonetheless, after a while, I grew accustomed to their presence in the background of our experience:

They capture intimate moments of Ron and I, together and in sessions with clients, offering talks, workshops and conferences throughout New Zealand, Australia and Europe, walking beaches and picking fruit and coffee in Hawaii, and leaning over the rails of a beautiful wooden yacht while spinner dolphins swim starboard, and turn to greet us eye to eye with giant dolphin smiles.

As wonderful a time as I'm having traveling a world I'd never seen or known, concurrently I'm discovering Ron has a trail of lovers in seemingly every country, or new ones to be found, and as I grow taut like a drum as the nights and days pile on, it dawns on me that all along I'd expected things would change. I'd considered poly an intensive lesson of sorts, not the final ultimatum, and certainly not this revolving door. I've assumed he'd find contentedness in the love we share. Why wouldn't he? We have a great time together, at least when it's just us, but those times are rare.

Still, I remind myself that I want to learn the lessons of Tantra and Sacred Sex. I want to be bigger than my emotions, have a life greater than the one I've known; I have to stick with this. So I turn inward, scream into my hands, punch pillows, own my anger and disgust, and imagine myself as a man with a cock, trying to find the place that just wants to fuck. Still, as much endless work as I'm doing, and as much as I think I'm aware, it seems my emotional reactions are progressively getting worse: now I'm reactive even when he's just *talking* about other lovers. In the heat of the moment, my mind can't tell the difference between what's real, and what are only the symbols and sounds of words.

But as we arrive into a river port in Budapest, my shoulders finally drop. We are scheduled to attend a fifteen-day cruise with his family along the Rhine and Danube.

No talks, no workshops, no young, available women. Just family, and a good lot of 'em: siblings, aunts, uncles, parents, and even a few cousins.

His mom, wiry with thin with painted lips and red-rimmed eyes framed in plastic lenses, sits behind the piano in the dining hall to sing old Hungarian songs while the family gathers around with glasses of red wine and scotch. Dad sits, watching his hands folded over a massive belly, lifting his eyes on occasion to scan the crowd and mutter something under his breath. Ron's the youngest of five, all of whom are on board. Jim is three years Ron's elder, a down to Earth computer techie, married for years to a woman who paints Picasso-esque house pets for a living. The eldest brother is Tommy: a dogmatic Christian with a compulsive lying problem and a penchant for stabbing at Ron's proclivities. I tend to keep a bit of a distance, after our last encounter in the steam room of the Temple:

The last person departs, and after several moments of silence pass, through thick steam I hear:

"So, how's it feel to be living in the House of Iniquity?" I said I was hot and made a hasty departure.

Ron's eldest sister is an acupuncturist, also married to the man that I'd find later that evening on top deck, pissing over the ship's railings, all the while wailing: "YO, ho, ho and a bottle of rum!"

The sister in the middle is Jenna, a year older than Ron, who I'd met briefly in the bustle of initial introductions, but I'd hardly noticed her. She'd been quiet and melted like camouflage into the background.

Upon our third day, we dock ship to tour the Slovakian capital before entering Vienna. Drizzling and cold, Ron and I stay on the ship and wave goodbye. Tommy's on the dock with the others, hooked up with headphones, ready for a guided tour. He gazes pitifully up at us, looking something akin to a walking condom in his translucent yellow raincoat with the hood tied taught around his rain-dampened face.

Hours later, Tommy shows up at the lunch table with a plate piled high with chicken, potatoes and vegetables, and sits across from Ron and I.

"The cathedral was SO awesome!" He says, too enthusiastic for his demeanor, shovels mashed potatoes into his mouth and chews, watching us as he peers over the rims of his glasses. He catches Ron's eyes, then mine.

"You guys really should have come. It's Sunday, you know."

"I sure wouldn't have wanted to miss that mass! *Such* a beautiful and uplifting sermon!" He says, wagging his head.

"Powerful! Wow. I'm *so* glad I went."

Ron asks why it was so amazing, what the sermon was about? We stop eating and watch Tommy in genuine interest.

Tommy stops chewing and takes a long pause and his eyes slide to the right. He looks back at us, then to his food, and trails a fork through his potatoes and scratches the back of his head with the other hand.

"Actually, I kind of just walked through. We didn't really hear a sermon."

I choke on my OJ.

Ron and Tommy finish their meals and rise to mingle with family while I bury my face in a book, until I hear Ron's voice, and look over to find a family drama going on at an adjacent table.

Mind your own business, Maya. I lean in closer.

Jenna's eyes are glossed over. Apparently, she's upset with Ron. Ron's in the corner with Jim, his arms crossed and head tilted to the side as he listens to his brother. Ron's mother wraps her arm around Jenna, squeezing her shoulder.

"It's the past," she says, patting Jenna's locks.

"We have to move past these things, you were both young. Why don't you two try to work things out?"

Jenna's slit eyes search the room, stopping at Ron, who raises his brows before he lifts his hands and shakes his head. Jenna turns back to her mother.

"He's never honestly recognized what he did!"

Ron slumbers off towards the cabins and I trot after him to catch up and ask what's going on. He's runs his hands over his head.

"Let's talk in our room."

We unlock the room and I plop down next to Bob, who's laid down and sighs with his palms over his eyes.

I wait.

"Jenna claims that when we were young, I tried to manipulated her into having sex." he says.

"What?" I jump up, my eyes darting the room.

"Well!" I glare, showing him my palms. "*Did* you?'

"Maya," he says, calm as a lamb. "I didn't manipulate a thing."

My heart pounds in my chest. I don't want to know this. *My God, has he been doing this kind of thing all along?*

I sit on the end of the bed, not knowing what to do, suddenly feeling like I'm sitting next to a monster.

"You really need to look at this!" I blurt.

"Don't you think you need to own your part and recognize how deeply this has affected your life, and Jenna's, I mean, the whole families! Shit Ron, this is the very work you do!"

"Maya, I've done plenty of work around this," he says, "I'm not the one that's upset here. She is. It's her shame and guilt she has to work through."

Ron sighs, covers his mouth with his hands and screams. His face turns bright red.

My fingers tap the sideboard of the bed as my eyes dart around the room. I want to jump out of my skin.

I would eventually be informed that sex didn't happen; Jenna got out as soon as she realized he was trying to seduce her.

But this is the same kind of response I've heard him say too many times to claims of transgression from others, lovers and women in workshops: their accusations are their own projections and a result of their repressed guilt, shame and fear around sex. But this incident really struck me. Ron often sounded like a broken record, interminably repeating the mantra of "guilt, fear and shame around sex," but now I seriously began to wonder if these words weren't borne from his own shame, denial and projections.

The whole thing's profoundly conflicting: on the one hand, his perceptions are so often correct, I've seen it so many times myself. On the other, just because there is projection, does that mean an accusation is not, at least in part, correct? It seems to me that Ron's method of handling accusations from women is akin to her pointing in horror at a burning man, screaming; "HIS HAIR'S ON FIRE!' But because she's upset about it, the fire isn't there.

The following morning, the incident seems forgotten, and I spend the day swinging wildly between compassion and repulsion, understanding and disgust. But I'm here. There's nothing I can do but be with what is and enjoy the rest of this ride as best I can.

We tour through the Ringstrasse of Vienna, the museums of Nuremberg, and a stunning Gothic Cathedral in Cologne, and return to the ship late afternoons to make love and emerge to delight in hearty German bread, olives, cheese, and fresh fish smothered in rich gravies.

After fifteen days on the river we reach the port of Holland, our final destination, and saying adieu to Ron's family, we rent a little car, and take off on our own towards Amsterdam. Parking on a quiet side road in town, we step out to walk through foggy, dampened streets. Movement within a window of a large, brick building catches our attention, one of twenty or so windows along its red brick face. A prostitute sits on display in each one, waiting to be chosen. My heart drops as I scan the street, no one around.

Not long ago I found prostitutes vile and dirty. I'd never seen past what I'd always been taught. But it's one area where attending conferences on Sacred Sex have altered my perspectives. I'd met several prostitutes who'd attended, and they were so often more grounded and authentic, albeit hardened, than the bindi and sarong wearing Tantrikas.

Many of them claimed to truly love their work, serving men that would not receive love or attention otherwise. In this context I could see them as deeply loving and compassionate women to offer themselves as they do. Yet for those who don't share such sentiment, participating through force or economic need, I can only imagine the nightmares they live, and the shame hits me how much prejudice and despise is cast towards these women. I'd considered prostitution several times myself to make ends meet. Another roll of the die and I might have been one of the women in those windows.

Ron and I come upon a sign in neon lights: 'Smokey's Coffee Shop,' with ad posters plastered over the windows from the inside.

"Must be the place." Ron says, grinning and ushers me in. We climb into stools at an empty bar and scan the decor until a husky, bald man with beaming blue eyes in a plaid shirt appears from the back, and without a word, hands each of us a menu: 'Blueberry Kush,' 'Afghani black', 'Nepali black', we earnestly look it over as if we'd know one from the next.

Just being here makes me want a cigarette. It's been a year since I bought any, but I order a single and pad my pockets for my blue lighter. Nothing.

"Maya." I look up. Ron has it in hand, flame already lit. *How'd he get my lighter?*

After Ron orders, the bartender disappears and returns with a crystal-covered bud and pack of rolling papers. I twist up a joint and hand it to Ron, who moments later, smiling and glassy-eyed, tells me he'll be right back. I start up a conversation with the bartender who's eyes dart over my shoulder and I hear a crash behind me, and crane my neck around to find Ron passed out cold on the floor, his hand on the lavatory doorknob, and turn back to the bartender with a brow raised.

"Potent stuff," I say.

"It happens." The bartender retorts with a wink, and hands me a small glass, telling me to place it under his nose. "It'll rouse him."

But the herb plays its tricks on me as well. As Ron rises and disappears into the lavatory my mind spins with dissent:

Honestly, barely a drop of respect remains for Ron. So why am I still here?

He's somehow managed to treat me both better and worse than any man I'd ever been with. He listens. He always wants me with him. He gives me lots of attention. He genuinely cares, at least about some things, and yet, he's the very impetus to my anguish and pain. But when things get rough, he's always reminded me:

"I cannot create the pain within you. It's yours to feel. It was already there."

Do I continue walking with a man who continually turns to batter me with a sledgehammer in my efforts to rise above the intensity of my emotional pain? Has my life not been challenging enough? How long must I continue Spiritual warfare within myself? Is this a path of self-abuse...or am I healing?

Is it the mystery and intrigue; my lack of assurance and desire to unlock the psychological puzzles around the nature of love, sex, and even Ron, that holds me here?

There was that dream with the rainbows I had in the beginning, and I saw them when we were on our tour through Australia. They were the very same ones. I've never seen double rainbows like that before.

Beyond all that, I'm traveling the world, being *seen* as a teacher, making lots of new friends, learning to be a 'Sacred Sexual Healer' and a 'Tantrika'... or am I?

Ron lumbers out of the loo, and I snap back into the present. We make it out of there soon enough, taking with us a small bundle to offer as gifts along the way, and head into Germany. Of course, until we saw the flashing lights, we hadn't considered the inevitability of being pulled over at the first roadblock over the border, seeing we had Holland plates.

Two officers approach, one on each side of the car, knock on our windows and immediately request we step out. They inform each of us in private that if we have any weed, it'd be best to hand it over, no problem, and they'd let us go. If not, they'll bring the dogs, and if they have to go through all that and find any, they'll be unpleasant consequences.

It's a no brainer. We've got barely more than a pinch and I have no doubt this is standard occurrence. I tell my officer there's some in the pocket of the black bag in the back seat...he's welcome to it. Meanwhile, apparently, Ron is informing his interrogator that we're clean. We have nothing. The officer on my side retrieves the pot, marches around the car, and hands it to the other officer who then dangles it before Ron's face.

The cop demands, "No pot?"

Ron shoots me a look, then deadpan to the officer and says, "That's her pot."

"*MY* pot!" I storm around the car and stand in front of Ron. "What the hell!" I yell. *"My* pot! What the hell are you talking about!"

Images of being stuck in some remote German prison with no one to help, dance through my head. Both cops remain silent as I pace before Ron.

HOW can this man POSSIBLY be a teacher of relationship!

"Um, Ma'am?" We both look up. One of the officers, forces down a bemused grin.

"If we catch either of you with marijuana over the border again, we'll put you under arrest. Is that understood?"

"Yes." Ron says.

"Ma'am?"

"Yes." I grumble.

We get back into the car and I glare at Ron.

"Maya, what was I supposed to do? You told him we had pot, they'd have let us go no problem if you hadn't said that." I fold my arms.

"You have no fucking balls." I say, and turn my head to fume out the window.

Chapter 22~ The Final Cut

Ron has one last client before we reach our final destination. Then, just a few weeks left and we'll be home. Her name is Gayle, and he's worked with her before. They'll session and we'll stay in her guest room for the night, and as we pull into her driveway, I gather myself and, as best I can, replace my 'I can't believe I've ever touched your slimy cock with a ten foot pole' mask, for a slightly more bright and cheery one in lieu of their impending session.

The door opens to a fiery redhead: lovely, open-armed, and delighted we've come. I'm annoyed to discover I like her as she ushers us into the kitchen, where heaping bowls, full of prepared salads, cheese and olives await us.

"Serve yourselves," she chirps with a rosy-cheeked smile.

She tells us over dinner that she works days at an elementary school, and in the evenings as a hospice director. She's intelligent, motivated and wonderful in every way, but no matter how delightful, I just can't seem to get myself to authentically feel happy within the looming potential that soon, she and Ron may very well be in her room, fucking like high school sweethearts on prom night. I just never know: sacred spot I can handle. Sex I cannot.

In fact, in the ever- impending doom I seem incapable of enjoying much of anything anymore.

And that evening as their session progresses and there's no escape from the sounds of pleasure reverberate through the walls, something in me breaks and I can't fake it anymore.

This whole thing has been nothing like I thought it would be. Somehow this dream of becoming a Sacred Sex Goddess, so mysterious, inviting and full of potential in the start, turned out to be more like a journey through the Valley of Darkness, or maybe just plain hell, something or other to that effect.

Is this truly any more *Sacred* and *Spiritual* than porn or prostitution or sex on cocaine (which, by the way, sex with Ron couldn't even touch:

angels had me exponentially orgasming on that stuff)... or any of your everyday, run of the mill, sex obsessed and dysfunctional relationship?

Besides, no matter how many times I do this, I feel like shit. I'm not learning compassion. I'm not watching my fear pain or jealousy disintegrate into a misty cloud of mauve. In fact, I think I'm even worse off emotionally than when I started.

So I'm just not conscious enough to be a big shot, polyamorous Tantrika.

Boo Hoo. I admit my guilt: I like sex with one person.

I pace the room, my mind racing. Moans rise; Gayle's singing the Carmina Burana.

Really, you're done? Seriously, after all this, you're just giving up?

When the noise finally ends, I battle with myself all the way to their door, where I timidly knock without knowing what to say. My heart pounds in my ears and I'm about to turn back when Ron's voice, sweet as pumpkin pie invites me in, so I creak open the door to find them naked under the covers, sitting up and smiling at me.

I might throw up.

I stutter: "Um, you guys all right? Do you need anything?"

I'm shaking like a third latte in an hour and clasp my hands to hide it.

Ron invites me to lay with them and I slump down into his arms for a moment, but demons are doing cannonballs in the murky water pit of my gut and the only overflow is through my tear ducts. Still, I have to remain intact for their session, so I rise up again and, hiding my face, say something stupid like:

"I'm glad the two of you had a good session."

I pull the door behind me, leaving a crack through which I feebly request Ron's presence sometime soon in the other room

I gaze at pictures of Gayle, family and friends hung on the wall by the stairs:

Gayle: twenty years younger at graduation. Gayle: smiling her rosy brilliance with two young girls, maybe her daughters.

Why can't I just be happy for her? Why can't I enjoy the fact that she's enjoying her sexuality, on whatever level, with Ron?

That night I sit next to Ron on the bed and release Niagara falls. I tell him I need a break. I'm falling apart, and totally repulsed with all of this sex. Besides, I've realized this morning I'm a good week past my period, and I'm never late. Seriously, I need to stop, I tell him. I'm sure it's the stress.

Ron looks me over and takes my face into his hands.

"This is it!" Chipper as if he was just handed the winning lottery ticket, "you're right on the edge! *Now* is not the time to go into separation, Maya, but rather if you're feeling that way, this is the time to *cultivate* your sex! You have to face your emotions and go into this *deeper* so we can strengthen our love! Let's go for the more!" he proclaims.

I stare into his eyes. That sounds about as appealing as gnawing on a turd.

My very soul is screaming.

"I just don't want this anymore, Ron. I want to go home." *Wherever that is.*

But that night I lay in bed after we have sex, during which I feign physical pain to keep brief, and stare at the ceiling.

Two weeks left. That's it. I can hold out until then. What else am I going to do, anyway? What if he's right? What if this really is the edge, and what if I can move past this? I know there's truth to the words he's said: attraction and repulsion are the cues, and I'm definitely repulsed. In fact, I think I hate him.

After having been together for over a year, Ron and I were back in Santa Fe. I'm sitting in a circle with Daka Chris and Ron on the back deck. An early winter chill is in the air. Chris pops a cigarette between his lips and tips his chin forward, inviting Ron or me to light it. I pat my pockets- empty- and turn my palms with a shrug. Chris turns to fish through the fanny pack resting behind him and comes up with a blue lighter.

"Hey!" I sit tall, spying the thin slice of red tape I'd wrapped around it a few days earlier.

"No wonder...you have it!"

Chris lights his smoke, casually tosses the lighter back into his fanny pack and turns back to me with a sneer. I can't help but love him for his audacious charm.

Chris is one of two men I'd been with over the course of this sexual journey with Ron. The other was Bob's cousin Jason, and behind that experience lurked the proverbial trying: trying to keep up, trying to be free and polyamorous, trying to create some kind of balance with Ron. It was just weird.

But being with Chris was a positive experience. Not just for pleasure, per se, but because he's a friend in which I'm attracted without all the strings and emotional attachment, our sex offered to me an embodied experience of remaining detached without jumping right into my usual pattern of ripping my heart out to set it down upon a silver platter, beating with my life-force and power, for a man to dance the tango upon if it were to his fancy and pleasure. At the same time, the act confirmed, there's just not as much pleasure for me without said emotional connection. Conclusion: I'm doomed, I guess.

I'd requested Chris to be present as I wanted a mediator for the ultimatum I was about to give Ron. We all sit, holding hands, and say a prayer. When we open our eyes, I tell Ron, I'm appreciative of all of the experiences he's brought into my life, traveling the world, workshops, conferences, an entire community... nevertheless, I'm beyond emotional exhaustion. I've stuck with his ways all of this time. Now I'd like him to try mine: my request is, starting now, he takes one month off of sleeping with other women. I'm painfully in need of space and time to gather myself and get back on my feet. I'm overcooked, toast, done.

Ron looks into the distance seeming to ponder, then to Chris, and shakes his head.

"I feel shackled." he responds, and gets up to pace in front of us.

"I won't be controlled by fear." He says.

I stare in disbelief, my eyes watching him walk about the room. I'm searching for humanity, connection, empathy, something. I'd thought this was a no-brainer, like none of this was actually real, this whole thing was a kind of spiritual testing grounds, some deep, crazy Tantric wisdom now to be revealed. I'd run way past the lines of my boundaries, flung open wide the drapes of my comfort zones. I'd stuck with it, all the way to the finish line. Hadn't I passed? Don't I get a sticker or a gold star, or something like *real* love and care from him now?

But it all was real, just as it was. Ron's incessant claims of love and convictions that I was his Beloved were only words, noises, they weren't going to somehow warp and transform the reality we'd been living into what I understood those words to mean. No magic fairy dust was going to change my ideals to his, simply because they were so fluffed up and decorated with Spiritual terms and appeared upon first glance, and with the help of some inspiring talk, performed with zeal and conviction, more loving or conscious. Experience showed me, his lifestyle wasn't necessarily any better or worse. It was just his, and I got caught up in it.

I think deep down, both of us were sure the other would eventually come to their senses and see the truth of our own convictions about love and relationship. Perhaps I'd always done this. Maybe everybody does.

I drop my eyes down to my hands, and the last of my tears falls for Ron.

I stalk by a woman in the living room without going out of my way to pay her the kind of attention I'd always given to Ron's lovers. Having fucked him while I was away on a visit with my mother, with no amount of care or respect to inquire about my feelings when she's well aware of the frailty of circumstances, I ignore her.

And when I'm in my bathroom brushing my hair and Ron walks in to stand behind me to watch our reflection in the mirror, I say nothing and continue brushing. He places his hands on his hips:

"Maya, you're terrorizing my lover!" he proclaims.

I see red and come completely undone. I swing around, and throw a fist directly into his diaphragm. He runs out of the bathroom as I cover my mouth and suck air, amazed at what I'd just done.

"Do you see what you've done?" Ron yells.

I don't know why I run after him apologizing. I've never hit anyone in my life.

That, in my mind, was the clear completion of my relationship with Ron and my training in Tantra and Sacred Sex.

The following afternoon, he finds me packing, he tells me that he knows I'll come back to him: he knows who I really am!

I pause and look up at Ron. *Is he serious?*

Ron's shaking, his hands in fists by his sides, and I get the sense that at this moment, he's transgressed to about a five year old.

"I know you Maya! I know you still love me!" he offers in an eerily child-like pitch.

I stare into my half-packed bag. This is when I'm supposed to see that he's finally cracked open, wide and vulnerable, and accordingly, comfort him. Certainly I know his condition. I'd seen it a thousand times in myself for over a year now. But every ounce of me is done with this.

"I'll always love you, Ron." I say and look him in the eyes.

"But you've made your decisions. I'm done with this now. If you don't mind, I'm trying to get out of here."

Several weeks later Ron calls me at my new home, not far down the road. He says the producers have requested my presence; they need at least an interview and a few good shots in order to create a decent closing for the film.

At first I refuse. I have no interest in promoting Ron's work. I've seen too much. But Ron reminds me he's already put a lot into the making of this, and then I just up and take off.

Out of obligation, I plaster a smile over my lips, show up, and speak with one of the producers. He assures me they'll do their best to be in integrity and present the story as it happened.

I'm just going to have to trust this one.

Ron's second request is that I go away with him for the weekend to the Grand Canyon. I say no. He needs to speak with me. I say no. No strings attached. "No!" My voice rises.

"Maya, I'd like to speak with you. I promise, there'll be no pushing for sex."

I pause. He wouldn't out right lie about that.

"Ok. Fine. I'll hear you out." I say. Besides, I haven't been to the Grand Canyon yet.

We stand at the front desk at a hotel overlooking vast canyons. Clearly he's seeking to impress, as the concierge hands him the key to the Presidential suite.

Ron sits next to me on the bed and opens a tiny velvet box. Inside is a beautiful ring, native style with turquoise set in gold and a diamond, displayed in shiny blue satin.

"Just give me a year." He says. "Things will be better, Maya. You're my beloved, and you should know, you'll never have to worry about being safe or having money again. You will always have that if you stay with me."

I try on the ring and admire it on my finger, and slide it off to hand it back.

"You know, all of this is really sweet, but I'm not going to marry you, Ron."

"It can be just you and me. I'm willing to be monogamous with you. Give it a few days, Maya."

He won't be satisfied unless I follow his directions, and truth is it's stunning. Guiltily, I want to feel what it's like to wear it, its weight on my finger, if even for only a few days. I slip the ring back onto my finger, admiring the luster of gold, turquoise and diamonds against my skin.

Over the following days, the consideration doesn't as much as arise as a potential option. I was well aware he wouldn't be capable of monogamy no matter what he now says. His words hold no integrity.

A few days later, I return to the temple and hand him the ring, just as I'd said.

"Now you have all the freedom you seek." I tell him.

I do as well. I'd met a new lover at a temple party on New Years Eve, just before I made my exit. He's flighty, non-committal and emotionally unavailable: i.e., I'm topsy-turvy, head over heels for him.

Apparently I haven't learned much. I need to nurture and heal myself, sprout some wings and be free from all of this.

And my like for the feel of that ring gave to me an idea:

A week later, I went out and bought a ring, climbed one of my favorite hills, and created a ceremony for myself. *With this ring, I chose union with myself, from this moment on.*

Chapter 23 ~ Deep Medicine

I'm driving through lush green hills and grape fields deep in Sonoma County, en route to my first Ayahuasca ceremony. It's my thirty-seventh, and this ceremony has been offered to me as a birthday gift from a lover who has been watching me over the past few months, growing ever more gaunt and tired. Since I left Santa Fe, I'd resorted to residence in my van after spending a bundle I'd saved for the purpose of a yoga training; a move in determination to take my healing into my own hands as well as a potential way to step away from Tantra and Sacred Sex.

I was good at it, being a Dakini. I'd found success there and had built a name for myself through my musings with Ron, yet sensual massage, like stripping, like sex, all have profound therapeutic qualities until you're enslaved to them for the money, then they turn to poison, instead. Every stroke of prostate and lubricated cock began to suck what little energy and integrity remained in the space between my cells. Oh, there were still the clients I could serve well without going there, however you can only teach authentically from the depths of your own well...and as things were going with my health, something had gone very wrong.

I pull into an empty space, soft with redwood needles, and the light of the full moon shines through high branches, casting perfect shadows along the path that leads to an old, cedar wood cabin. I climb up a stairwell to find people bustling between a long, wrap-around deck nestled with redwood boughs, and a large candle-lit room.

Inside, several people are setting up nests of pillows and blankets in a semi-circle around a stout man sitting in the center. Black hair protrudes from a yellow cloth wrapped around his head. His lips move silently in prayer while he unwraps ceremonial pieces, placing them, one by one, all around him.

I step in and claim a spot under a window on the far side of the room, and sit to take in the activity in preparation for ceremony.

Two women enter the room and introduce themselves as volunteers for the night. The eldest is May, a woman with thick blonde dreadlocks, who kneels down beside the shaman and exchanges words with him in Spanish, then rises to inform us that we'll begin in about twenty minutes.

"You'll all come up, one by one, to drink your first cup. If you've never tried this medicine, know that it's extremely bitter and thick. You want to drink your cup down fast. After an hour or so, they'll be opportunity for a second, but remember, best to take that only if you really don't feel much at all from the first. This medicine is strong and it can sneak up on you. It does happen, however, that for some on their first try, you won't feel anything, while others will go completely off on a journey."

The shaman pours liquid from an opaque brown bottle into another, wipes both rims, folds his cloth, and sets it upon a small, embroidered box.

"All night, we'll be here." May says. "If you have to use the bathroom, or need another bucket, or anything, just raise your hand and one of us will come to support you."

She looks over her shoulder and gestures towards the Shaman.

"If any of you haven't yet met Oscar, he's our amazing Shaman here to guide you through this ceremony."

Oscar looks up, nods, and grins; displaying a two-tooth wide gap on the left side of a bright smile, and turns to speak something in Spanish to May. She returns a nod and turns to elucidate.

"Oscar is saying the most important thing to remember, if you're struggling," she pushes air down with her hands, "is to simply relax, and let go."

The second volunteer is a quiet girl in her mid-thirties, with gentle brown eyes.

She places a small, orange bucket in front of me and kneels down to meet my eyes.

"You have everything you need?" she whispers.

"I think so." I say, smiling, and take her hand in appreciation.

She rises and makes her way to the next person. *She's volunteered to change vomit buckets all night, surely she's got wings beneath her shirt.*

I'm left staring at my bright orange bucket. The purging aspect of this medicine is what I've felt most tentative about. I simply can't fathom throwing up in a room full of people, they doing the same. I lean back into a resting position, and then sit up toward the bucket to estimate its correct positioning.

Oscar lights candles all around him, illuminating his shiny black eyes, and May inform us it's time to go up to Oscar, one by one, to receive a cup.

The man next to me reaches out his hand to introduce himself.

"Peter," and hands me a leaf.

"It's Coca," he says, meeting my gaze with bright blue eyes that look all the more stunning against his curly red beard and shaved head. "It's nice to go with the medicine," he says with a grin.

"Cool, thanks!" I say, and chew. It's clean and earthy; I'm intrigued this is the origin of a drug that once held me so tight in it's clutches.

"Have a good journey!"

"You too!" I say with a nod, comforted by the kindness of my neighbor.

When my turn arrives, I scurry to Oscar and kneel down before him. Black, shining eyes meet mine, he gestures in prayer and hands me a tiny ceramic cup that I lift to my mouth. Thick tar creeps down my throat, making me gag, but I force it down and hand the cup back, with a grimacing bow and slink back to my seat.

I've heard so many stories about this medicine, people receiving messages, seeing entities, or traveling distant universes. I'm just hoping to feel good again. Still, it might be cool to meet an entity, I think, I don't know, maybe not actually. I hope this isn't scary.

An hour or so passes as I sit, waiting in the dark without noticing much minus odd, squishy noises, exaggerated yawns, creaks and whispers. But then, a peaceful, melodious voice arises; Oscar has begun an angelic song. Resting my head back, my insides feel more clean and open. Oscars voice soothes me and I slip silently into another world. Black and white patterns arise that zigzag, twist, flash and vibrate like light against a fan. Shapes appear and expand into concentric circles, one layer after another, ever growing in a cacophony of rhythm where I have choice to remain or emerge at will.

Oscar completes his song and I open my eyes into a dark room of loud whispers and creaking wood. Grey shadows lurk about the room, trails following behind them. Ankles and toes crack, sniffs, yawns, and crickets. Moonlight falls into the windows and I hold out my hand to watch the shadows crawl over it. A soft voice arises: May.

"It's time for a second cup if anyone would like."

I rise up and wobble to Oscar with one other person and we each drink a second.

Returning once again to my seat, I close my eyes and snuggle into blankets. Oscar shakes a rattle, plays melodious flute and again, begins to sing. Peace flows like a wave through me and once again I find myself traveling through another domain: thick grey fog becomes superimposed with colorful dots and spinning wheels. My head falls forward and then rolls back, and I suddenly realize, I'm moving on no volition of my own. My chin jerks suddenly to my left shoulder, then to the right, and then falls back to rest; *a cosmic neck adjustment!* I can't help but laugh. It's like ethereal hands are moving me, but without touch!

My stomach is pushed in on one side. I open my eyes and look down at my body. Indeed, there's an indent, and movement as if something is manipulating me from the inside. I grin and look around the room, hoping someone else might be getting a gander at this, but everyone's in their own process.

A ripple runs under my skin, tickling like insects running up my spine, and I reach an arm around to try and feel what it is, but there's nothing. Bluntly, I'm pushed to the side, giddy in this absurdity. I'm possessed! My arm suddenly flies up behind my head so my elbow's pointing up and my hip shakes wildly. I'm giggling, totally comfortable as my whole body twisting and turning, being pushed and pulled from all directions. *This must be alien massage!*

Bliss flows through me, and a voice, my own voice, arises in my mind: *"She moves you as She moves you."* Apparently she does!

"She moves you as She moves you." The mantra repeats and I relax and fall into its melody. *"She moves you as She moves you,"* the words repeat in an endless cycle while another layer of thought overlaps, *"all perfect, Divine, Sacred, the knowledge lives within our genes, the Earth, plants, and trees. She moves you as She moves you."* My hip rolls over and

I sprawl out, half up on my pillow, twisted and shaking. "She moves you as she moves you."

I gaze at my hands and light suddenly switches on in my mind, I suddenly understand: She, God, Divinity, Consciousness, is and has always been moving me! It has never been myself, I, separate and alone. She's showing me that now! She is what moves everyone! *That* is what this is about, God and I are inseparable. We, everything, everyone, have always and ever will be One!

The song stops and all is silent, a void between cracks, creaks and crickets, until a monstrously amusing flapping sound breaks the silence. It takes me a moment to comprehend: someone's purging.

That's what I was afraid of! I fall apart laughing. Another burst follows, then several at the same time, the entire room must be losing their cookies!

Still, as fast as I'd found mirth, so just as swiftly a wave of compassion flows over me, and I find myself holding each one of them, quietly from a distance.

Oscar begins another song.

This one is staccato, marching, and my breath runs shallow. Sharp patterns and unknown shapes, solid, black and white checkers, stars and pinwheels spinning fast, growing ever larger, overtaking me. I don't know where I am, I'm afraid, I don't like this place. But a deep but barely discernible voice tells me I have a choice:

Face this and keep going, or I can distract myself and get out of this.

But this is why I'm here. I have to face it. Patterns grow larger, damp and vibrant with color, overtaking me as I narrow, suffocate and contract. My stomach ties into knots. Pure fear overwhelms me, tightening until I can no longer breathe. Colors squeeze into a spiral in a tight center below, pure terror. I can't open my eyes, but I have to throw up, NOW! My hands grope blindly for the bucket and I find the rim and hold on both sides and my head flies forward, but there is only boundlessness space. Oh my god, I'm going to miss. I fall into the spiral contraction, squeezing.

Silence.

Void.

Nothing.

Where am I?

The world opens into a thousand pink lotuses, each petal unfolding, one after the next blossoms open, worlds expand upon worlds. Bliss flows though me in beautiful, bright oceanic waves: colorful, blissful, endless silence.

My sacrum shakes and pulses, becoming more intense. I may orgasm right here and now. My body is still moving about, but I rise fast, leaving, until I no longer know where my body is. I move up into the atmosphere of the earth, through stars. I look down to see Earth below me, shrinking smaller as I travel further away, into silent blackness.

I am Goddess.

Here, the void is endless bliss. I am nothing and everything, endless in the silence of perfect Samadhi.

There is no need. No physical sensation, no desire, no fulfilling of gratification: only blissful nothingness. She is vibration, thought, breath, action, reaction, manifest...perfect, endless bliss. Earth and all its drama and activities are meaningless, irrelevant, all of it both perfect and ludicrous. Nothing matters in the least, and yet it all matters: every thought, every word, every moment, every second creates all that is; perfect contradiction, Divine paradox. Life is to be enacted responsibly, without being serious about it at all.

I have no care if I ever were to return: although, the thought arises:

My mother has already lost a son, so if given choice I will be responsible and be there for her, yet if my fate is not to return, so be it.

I remain in stillness until images arise: friends, beloveds, smiling eyes, a wave of gratitude for all creation and experience fills me, and I slowly return to by body.

I'm sitting forward, comfortable, with my legs crossed, my head... face down in a bucket. I rise up shaking, and realize I'm about to explode. I need to pee, orgasm, shit and vomit all at the same time. I've never felt so full. I can't move, but I must.

I raise my hand and May seems to arise from nowhere. I can't talk, but she seems to know what to do and pulls me up. I peek into my bucket on the way: a tiny drop of spittle.

I stagger out of the bathroom dazed and shaking like a leaf. Through the windows I spy the rest of the attendees, smoking on the deck, and May comes over and places her hand on my shoulder.

"You had quite a journey, you're one of the last. Can I take you outside?"

"Yes please, I'd love that." I say.

She directs me to a wooden chair on the deck and that's when I realize how high I still am. Ethereal grid lines weave like fishing line between the trees like I'm living in an Alex Grey painting. Peter squats down next to me and shakes out a cigarette, which I gladly accept.

"Oh thank God." I say, spying his watch. "What time you got?"

"Almost four in the morning." He says. I've already been out a good hour and a half."

I bring the cigarette to my lips and Peter clicks on a flame. I take in the smoke, deep and long, and exhale swirling tendrils that fade away.

"Oh that's so nice." I say.

"You took a second, must have been intense." He says.

I push my fingers into my temples, scrunching my face.

"Intense, yeah, I'm not so sure that second cup was my wisest choice."

I meet Peter's stunning blues, shaking my head.

"Not in my most drugged out, fucked up days, had I ever woken with my head in a bucket."

Chapter 24 ~ When Life feels like a Movie

Several months later, I'd driven across the States to land at the Temple and rest for a few days after receiving an email from Ron. He'd invited me to join on his tour through Australia, from where he'd written, and later, to travel on to New Zealand. He's still holding onto the idea that I'm his partner, and wants me to come, just come see how I might feel at this point. He says things are different. If I came back into his life, he'd stop being with other lovers. If it's not right, I go my own way, but he thinks it is. What is there to lose, he asks, isn't it worth giving us one last try?

Under any other circumstances, I wouldn't so much as bat an eyelash. But instead, I responded to his letter because, after three years, I remain sick with no signs of improvement, and I have to admit, against all logic and reason, it feels as if all this has something to do with our relationship: mainly because, since I left, I'd both grown sick, and he's uncannily hovered, like some phantom, lurking in the background of my experience. I've tried what I can, doctors, acupuncture, Chinese medicine, Sacred medicine, nothing has completely helped, and after three grueling years of illness and exhaustion, I have to face the reality that I'm completely out of juice and I might not be getting any better. If that's the case, I owe it to myself to experience something new, see if there is a place where love still shines through the hearts of people: maybe Bali, India or Peru. Whatever has held me in illness and confusion has to end. The invites been made. What I do now feels like a matter of life and death, so I sell my van for a ticket.

Ron and I stroll through a thick bush path in New South Wales, giant white cockatoos screeching overhead. We'd always loved hiking through desert and forest together. After these last few years, it's good to see him again. I watch him while he walks and he does indeed seem to be a little less chaotic and spun.

After our walk, he drives us to a resort close by where he's showing the completed documentary, which is exciting: I've yet to see it in its final edit.

That evening we join the group and splay ourselves over couches and pillows, the lights are dimmed, and I lay my head into the crook of Bob's arm, as the film's title appears center screen:

'Tantric Seduction: The Dance of Maya.'

I lift my head and look dumbfounded at Ron, who lifts his brows and his free hand as if to say, 'Gosh, I have no idea how they came up with that name!'

I'd assumed, since my leaving, I'd barely be in the film at all.

Still, as the movie plays through, I'm impressed. The producers captured the story well, although the events portrayed are hardly flattering to Ron and his work, in fact I'm surprised, for his sake, he'd want to present it at all. During the last quarter of the film, I find myself being filled in on what occurred after I left the Temple.

Ron is on the screen with a client, both of them naked in bed. There before me, I watch Ron perform a Sex Magic ritual to call me back into his life.

I lay there blinking at the screen.

Certainly I'd known he'd always considered me as his partner. But this- quite literally-added a whole other dimension to the story.

As the film comes to completion, I float in some strange world between relief and shock: relief in that the producers had portrayed the story for what it was, I might have, instead, been edited into the Tantra, Sacred Sex poster child. *There is a God.*

Shock because I can't quite wrap my mind around Ron's use of Sex Magic to call me back into his life. Here I am, and I want to get as far away from this psychotic little obsession as fast as humanly possible.

Fortunately, one of Ron's more reasonable and grounded lovers is present, one quite respected in the field, and the following day, I request she stand in as witness and mediation, for our final ritual.

The three of us sit and I explain clearly to Ron that I want him to let go completely. (I thought we'd done this already in Santa Fe). No more pulling. No more Sex magic ritual in my name. Ron is not, nor will ever be, my partner, nor my beloved. Soon he would be in New Zealand, I would travel to Bali, and we'll begin fresh with our own lives again.

Initially, Ron would not agree, leaving me sleepless that night in fear that the presence of his hungry ghost in my life would never end, however the following day, with some hours of discussion with myself and his other lover, he finally made agreement. Our ritual was finally complete.

Chapter 25 ~ Bali Dreamin'

Two weeks out of Oz, I arrive in beautiful Bali, a place known for its loving, gentle people as well as its magical healers; two birds with one stone, as they say. I'd gathered a few hundred dollars at the workshop with Ron, in hopes they'd be my last offerings of sensual massage, but hell... if this were what it takes.

Surely the money won't last, but Ubud, the town in which I've landed is also known for its yoga, perhaps I'll find a job. Whatever the case, I haven't been able to make it in the States. Something, somewhere, has got to give.

I settle into a bungalow and fish out a slip of paper with the name of a Shaman; 'Ketut,' scribbled upon it, recommended from a new Aussie friend. She assured me, as she handed over the square of green paper, it's not the same Ketut, 'Ketut Leer,' sought out from 'Eat, Pray, Love', whom I'd come to discover within later musings, had gained the nickname, amongst some of the Balinese anyway, as Ketut Liar. Was it true, or were the Balinese that told me so, simply jealous? A woman with an Asian twang answers the phone, "Herooow?"- Ketut's translator. We set up an appointment.

As I walk down the streets of Ubud, incense wafts deliciously from the entrance of every family compound, laid atop tiny servings of yellow rice, flowers and candies set in hand weaved grass baskets, and left as offerings for the ancestor Spirits and the Gods. Bougainvillea, frangipani, palms and bananas grow in every yard. Motorbikes and cars bustle along the streets and on every corner, women carry baskets of fruit, knives, and sarongs for sale upon their heads.

I show up at the Shaman's door: "I'm Anna, an' dis Pak Ketut" she bows. Ketut's a tiny man with amber eyes, a broad nose and very dark skin.

"Come, sit." Anna directs me to the front porch of their house, where I explain to her my plight while Ketut smokes, expressionless, as she relays to him my statements.

Anna looks at me and says; "Ketut vewy intewigent," she waves a tiny finger, "but one curse- no can learn Engwish." Anna giggles. I smile with her, but start to wonder if this is such a good idea.

Ketut puts out his cigarette in a coconut ashtray and stands.

"Ok, Silhakan," he says. Anna ushers me in, closes the door behind us and ascends the stairs.

"Ketut get me when you done." She says, winks, rounds the corner and disappears.

Ketut gestures for me to lie down on a mat on the floor. I have no way to communicate with this man.

"Take off" he says, pointing at my shirt, and walks back to the kitchen.

I lay there in my bra and crane my neck to find him opening a young coconut, which he brings back with him, prays over it, adds something to the water and leaves it to sit. Ketut kneels by my feet, looks me over with some huffing of breath, and points at my bra.

"Off" he says. *Ok, this is weird.*

Tentatively, I take of my bra and lay there half-naked. Ketut takes one of my feet, and begins to rub his thumbs along the edges of my bones, working his way toward the top of my foot and over my ankle. He seems to know every sensitive spot, and tends to hang out there, repeatedly rubbing over and over again, sending me on edge, and I doing my best to breathe through it. He works his way up my leg bones and deep into my inner thigh and just by my groin, pressing hard. I stifle screams. Whoever defined these people as gentle is *terribly* misguided! Tears well.

'Hot?' He asks.

I look at him,

"Tidak." No. (I know two Indonesian words; yes and no)

"No," I say, "not hot."

He presses again- more wrenching pain. I pull back, every muscle taught.

"Hot?" he asks again. I'm sweating profusely, but it's from pain, not from heat.

"No" I say. Annoyed. A tear slips down my cheek.

Then it dawns on me. *Hurt. He's asking if it hurts!*

"YES! YES IT HURTS!"

Oh my God, YES HURT! I get excited for relief. Ketut meets my eyes, nods, smiles, and continues. Apparently, we're doing this regardless of the excruciation.

I'm soaked in sweat at the end of the hour when he finally stops, gets up, and retrieves for me the coconut he'd prepared at the beginning.

"Drink." He says.

When we finally emerge from the torture chamber and Anna appears from seemingly nowhere, we step back out to the deck. Cool air brushes against my skin, and Ketut hands Anna and I cigarettes, as if he knows I'd smoke, and we all sit, sucking tobacco while discussing the session:

I'm concerned about what I discovered in Australia, I tell her.

The whole story is tying together, my sickness, exhaustion, Ron's perpetual lingering in the background, is it possible that his Sex Magic was the source of the illness and exhaustion the last three years?

Anna speaks to Pak and he nods.

"Don' worry," he says, and speaks a few words in Indonesian to Anna. She turns to translate.

"Don't worry about magic any more," she says. "Ketut has rid you of the problem."

And a miracle began.

Ever so slowly, as if a veil was lifting, the fog began to dissipate: my energy was returning.

I saw Ketut twice. The second time there was barely any pain, same movements, little pain. He gave me another potion at the end of our session, and told me to integrate fruit back into my diet again (vegetables and rice were the only thing my body could tolerate for the last three years.) Begin there... walk step by step.

"Now you awake, go do you work," Ketut said.

I stroll past pink and orange bougainvillea, cascading over moss-covered, rock walls of the compound I pass, still tingling from the loving connection of my morning session with an ex-pat client. I smile in realization that it's been a year, almost to the day, since my last sensual massage. A motor ceases several feet behind me and I gaze over my shoulder. A Balinese man, striking with long black hair streaked with grey and bejeweled around his neck and fingers, pulls up on the opposite side of the road. Our eyes lock.

"Hello," he says in a gentle, knowing tone. I stop in my tracks, *Medicine man*, and turn towards him.

"Hello," I return with a smile. He holds my gaze with wise, black eyes.

"Apa Kabar," I say, just to say something, and walk towards him. I don't know why. He looks me up and down, his brow furrowed with stern inquisitiveness and the jutting, downward turned lower lip of Native Americans.

"Come," he lifts his hand and nods towards an iron gate across the road.

"My house, we talk there."

Following his direction, I find my own subservience odd, but my curiosity is rather impervious to the stance of reason and logic. It may be dangerous, but at the same time I think it's what keeps the sparkle in my eye.

He invites me into a single, disheveled room; there's a poster of Hatha Yoga postures on the left sidewall, and on the same side, an altar covered with ceremonial pieces, offerings and a red and golden Balinese dragon mask. Offering baskets of every shape and size are piled on metal shelving on the right wall. There's a wooden chair, several musical instruments by the door, a long matt on the floor, and upon a countertop is an open coconut, a tiny vase of water with a half open lotus, incense, and a pack of Garam cigarettes; *Definitely a healer.*

"What you name?"

"Maya."

He smiles and a single cough of a giggle escapes him.

"Good Hindu name." he points to the mat in the middle of the floor. "Sit there."

He stands by the chair on the far side of the mat, grabs the pack of cigarettes, pulls one and tosses the pack back. I sit before him, and pull off my pack, curious what this is about.

"My name Dewa." He looks me up and down while he smokes.

I wait.

"What wrong wit you eye?" He points a finger under my left eye, tracing a half moon shape, squints, sits straight, grunts, and directs me to stand. He raises his arms out to his sides, and shakes his hand around my body: the rings on his fingers clacking and clicking together as he traces up and down each side, then turns me to face away from him and lifts my hands. I'm facing a Shiva lingam and my hands are in a position of praise to it.

Oh, this is rich.

Dewa wraps a dark hand round my shoulder and pushes a finger into the flesh at the underside of my collarbone.

"Hurt?" He asks. I flash back to my experience with Ketut.

"No," I say, giggling, "this does not hurt."

"Good" he says, and presses in, which pushes me backwards. Awkward, I lean against the pressure, trying not to fall back into him. But he releases his hold, and then goes for the opposite shoulder, tipping me back the same way. This time I lean so far back I have to step back with my left foot before I fall over. He releases again, takes my hips with both hands and moves me just slightly in a way that sends me bending forward.

I'm starting to wonder what's really going on, but the Balinese healer thing is an anomaly I wish not to disrespect with skepticism and misguided questions.

He's still moving my hips and I'm now bent all the way forward, my hands on the floor. I think he's pressing his pelvis against me.

Wait, does he have a hard-on?

Then, he takes his foot and nudges each of my legs so I spread them open and he's still pressed against me.

I'm actually amused at this point rather than frightened, but I do wonder how far he's going to go with this. Shouldn't I be freaking out?

He exhales, grunts, and tilts my pelvis forward in a way that sends me standing straight again.

I look over my shoulder at him.

"Do ya think I'll live?" I ask.

He's not amused, and turns me towards him so now we are eye-to-eye, warrior-to-warrior, breathing each other's breath.

I'm not afraid of you, which thought makes me realize I might just be a little scared. But I remain in his gaze and am amazed at how comfortable I am considering the picture here now being drawn. Again, Dewa lifts my hands, and we stand facing one another until he suddenly lets go of my hands and wraps his arms around me as if he's suddenly transformed into a five year old, and reaches for his incense and lighter. I shake my head, my mouth ajar in bafflement.

His hands retract and he lights an incense stick, suddenly giggling.

OK, so I'm totally being fucked with.

I'm embarrassed I've let this go so far, let myself be a stupid white tourist toy, but what to do, this is certainly entertaining, even if I am being made the fool. Regardless, somehow I still know that I'm safe.

He's serious again and runs an incense stick all around my body, then throws the incense to the ground by an offering on the floor and takes his cigarette and tells me to lie down on his bed.

Here we go. I'm no longer amused, but heck, I've already gone this far.

I hit the bed and ask a little uncomfortably; "belly up or down?"

He signals a flip with his hands with a cigarette hanging from his mouth and I turn over on my belly and look up to him for reassurance. He signals another flip and I giggle and turn over, "*this* way?"

I lie there on my back and fumble around uncomfortably trying to find where to put my hands. He sits down on the wooden chair and smokes.

After a few minutes he says; "I think you eye betta," and clears his throat and burps loudly several times, one after the other, as if releasing something.

We talk a few minutes and he asks "Where you stay?"

"Pengosekan," I say. "You know Made' painter? Next door to there."

Why am I telling him this?

"Yes." he says "I know, everyone know me dere."

He smokes and tells me a story about some tourists and a driver, but I'm distracted and start thinking about getting out of here, and ends his statement with: "...some time I not so normal."

I look up. He squints, leans his face forward.

"You know- norMAL?"

I sit up and contemplate a moment and retort, "Well..." I chirp, "I'm not so normal either."

Apparently he really likes this because he's grinning ear to ear and jumps down from his chair like a child and lies next to where I'm sitting. I lie down too and we talk more and he wraps an arm around me, and kisses me.

"Hey!" I say, and turn my head away.

This guy is completely bonkers!

He tells me he loves me.

Now he loves me!

This is so over the top that I have to play it out. Shaman or not, he's tiny. If it goes too far, I squash him. He is kind of cute. I let him kiss me, once.

He lifts his head.

"One, two, tree, four..." he whispers, and points to nothing in the air with each number. "five, six..."

He jumps up and reaches up his arms

"Sefen!" He circles his hand in the air.

"I never see dis before! Sefen line...sefen Spirit! Never before like dis!"

He's exasperated and gets up off the bed and lifts his shirt and looks down, revealing the wrap of his sarong and belly.

"Dey make hot- sweating!"

His body is healthy and beautiful; I'm a bit surprised. Surely he's at least late fifties. Instinctively I bring my hand to his belly. His skin is blazing.

"You *are* hot!" I say.

He brings his shirt back down and slowly lifts himself back onto his chair and stubs out his cigarette. My hands and feet tingle. As if by instinct, he brings a hand down and holds the instep of my left foot.

"Good, it coming out."

"Bad spirit?" I ask, a little sarcastically.

He looks at me, nods his head and smiles.

"Not so much."

He pulls another cigarette from his pack and lights, exhales hard and grunts. I've grown accustomed to this; Balinese men hardly ever inhale fresh, clean air.

"You no need teacher," he chimes in. "I like 'dis too. People say I am healing. I am teacher. No. I not healer. I not teacher. I not promoting. Only they know. They come if need. I don't know."

I don't know what to say to this and sit up, wobbly and out of sorts. Something in me feels very altered from spending time with this man, and I'm not altogether sure it's a good thing.

I tell him I have to go and start pulling my stuff back together. He juts his chin out.

"You leave phone nomor. I want see you again."

I fish through my bag, pretending there's no phone, and look at him, raising my brows and shrug my shoulders.

"I don't have my phone, but if you give me your number, I'll text after I get home."

He writes his information and hands me a slip of paper. I hug him, telling him to take care. I'll see him again, and walk out.

That was weird. Probably I won't.

I make it to my motorbike: pink with a splashing heart decal at the front. I slide on my helmet and sit for a moment, contemplating the day.

That night when I slide into the covers, I think that maybe tomorrow, I'll text. He says he wants to see me again. Perhaps this is how I can learn about Balinese healing.

I slip into a dream.

I've been visiting with a married couple in a trailer home. I don't know how I got here, what town this is, or even how much time's gone by. All I know is I'm on my way out. The tension in the air's so thick you could slice it, wrap it... take it to go. Art, the husband, is an average guy: stalky with dirty blond hair, grey-blue eyes, and the kind of blonde-red lashes that make a man appear thoughtful and kind.

As for his wife, I've never met her. I don't even know her name.

She's standing inside by the open window at the front of the trailer. She's thin and wiry with short, peroxide blonde, soccer mom hair, icy blue eyes, and heavy on the mascara. I'm standing outside on the stairs at the base of the trailer and looking up at her. I can't hold it in any longer. My hands fly into the air.

"What! Tell me. What is it? What's wrong?"

She cups a hand over her mouth and turns away. Tears well and pore over, streaming down her face.

"I don't want another woman to steal my husband!"

She sobs and wipes her tears with the inside of her wrists.

Art looks at his hands.

My heart sinks.

Red-rimmed eyes meet mine and she reaches her hands out. Suddenly we're in an embrace. I coddle her like a child, running my hands through her hair, resting my face into the top of her head, stroking her cheeks.

"I will never do that to you." I say, holding her in my arms.

"Never. You're safe. You are so loved."

Roosters crow: one, then another, endlessly calling into the distance. I drift in and out of sleep: this woman's pain penetrating through me each time I awaken. My palm rests on my forehead.

Then, a memory: I'm twenty-two, sitting at a bar in Durango, Colorado that smells of stale beer and steak fries. Saloon double doors swing shut behind wranglers and cowboy boots, the last customers of the night walk out.

The bartender watches me with a cocky smile and sharp blue eyes as he wipes glass mugs clean and sets them to dry, one by one, on a white bar towel. We've been flirting boldly for months, but it's always been in the safety of the crowd.

He leans in close onto his elbows, weaves his fingers together, his eyes across from mine. He's always served me attentively, watched me attentively, wanted me attentively. He says my name.

'Stay through closing. Drinks on me.'

I meet his eyes, smile and search through my bag for a pack of cigarettes.

'Ok. But just one.' I say.

Rick mixes a strong Long Island, and dips into it a tiny blue umbrella with Chinese script, sets down a napkin, the drink, and slides them before me.

'For the lady.' He winks.

Usually, my flirtations were reserved for when his girlfriend Shelly wasn't at the bar, Shelly manages the place, but last week, I don't know what happened, I was in a mood I guess. She's stocky with feathered, medium length hair, and brown eyes that were glaring at me from behind the bar. Rick said something that made me laugh, I don't remember what, and Shelly shoved in front of him.

"It's time for you to go," she said, "you're cut off."

Three quarters of a mug of ale still sat on the bar. I grabbed it, glaring at the three of her in front of me and drank it down, then smacked my lips and turned to drum up a conversation with the guy next to me.

I hadn't noticed she'd stormed around the bar until she was dragging me off the stool with a fistful of my hair, pulling me on a slow motion crawl on all fours across the floor. The door opened, and cold winter air, brushed over my face, then cement as I rolled onto the dark, empty sidewalk.

I shouldn't be here tonight. But right now, I'm too drunk to care.

Rick busies himself counting the money, wipes down the bar and saunters off to close the curtains in front. I fish through my purse for a triangular folded paper and set it on the bar along with a blade and a heart-shaped mirror with a plastic, golden frame.

Rick returns, and seeing me, grins and shakes his head, sets down a bottle of golden whiskey and a short glass onto the bar. I tap white powder out, onto the mirror and slide the blade through the pile, cutting two long, thick lines. Rick pours himself a whiskey, and steps around the bar.

When I'm done cutting out lines, I run my fingers along the edge of the blade and lick them, shooting Rick a glance. One side of his lip curls up.

He pulls out of his pocket a ten-dollar bill, and rolls it into a tight straw.

"Thank you, darlin'." He says, and leans himself forward, meets the bill to the mirror, presses a thumb over a nostril, and follows the line to the end.

I take a cigarette roll between my fingers, loosening a half an inch or so of tobacco and tap it out, bring it to my lips, suck powders into the empty space, lift my head, pull it from my mouth, and secure it with a twist.

'Cokey smokey,' I say with a wink, setting it aside, and receive back the bill to snort what remains.

Rick runs his fingers along my cheek. I take up the cigarette and light it, trying to distract. I never intended to act on the flirting. He's given me attention, and I've given it back, but for me it's always just been fun and free drinks. But, here we are, and he's leaning forward to kiss me- and why not? I go along with it.

When we part his eyes search mine before he turns to ponder the display of bottles behind the bar, then rests his chin in his palm. He wants out of this place, out of this town, out of the life he's been living for way too long.

We have sex on the bar's red leather couches. I can't say I much enjoy it: cold and not at all intimate. I don't know why I'm here. I don't know why I'm doing this.

At five am, Rick and I were in his truck, twenty minutes out of town, ready to leave everything behind, all of it. But Rick sighs, stops the car, and turns the ignition off before he rests his brow onto the wheel, and rocks his head side to side.

'We can't do this.' He says.

I don't peel my eyes open until sometime past eight. *Some things hardly change, but hey, I'm sober now, anyway.* The shades drawn, the house dark and quiet, I notice with some distaste, my belongings strewn about the place. Inspired with a task, I stretch long like a cat, slide out of bed and find homes for fugitive pieces of wardrobe. Dressed and clean, I peer into the mirror: brown, low, collar dress that hugs my slim hips- rarely do I wear feminine attire. Surely I'd fare better in the eyes of the public if I did. Satisfied, I slide a pack round my shoulders, unlatch the doors, and pull them open. From the corner of my eye, a black trajectory, one I identify as cockroach, flies straight at me, lands smack dab in the center of my chest, slides between my breasts, and scampers lighting fast down to my belly before I can register a scream.

The black thing smacks down with a damp thud onto the floor. My eyes follow. Between my feet, a lizard, frozen in place, stares up at me, then scurries underneath my desk and is gone. I deflate, *Thank God it wasn't a cockroach*, and step out to place my bag on the outdoor bench on the east-facing veranda that opens to a stunning view of rice fields and jungle: my impetus for this rental. *Thank You Divinity!*

Remembering to open the curtains, I step back inside and pull them wide.

I freeze. There, on the far side of the lawn, stands Made, cigarette in hand, looking directly at me...

Several months later, I'd find myself hiding in tall grass, watching young Balinese boys flying kites by the river. I'm out of money in a foreign country, tears falling and begging the same questions I always have:

Who am I? Why am I'm here? What am I supposed to be doing?'

Just then, iridescent blue catches my eye, a tiny candy wrapper, stuck between thick blades of grass.

'*Relaxa,*' it says, in bold, yellow text.

Relax. Isn't it amazing: at thirty-eight, I can't honestly say I've ever done that. The message- simple, pure, and clear- trickles like life's elixir into my Kentucky fried nervous system.

I've played the Spirituality game; the quest for love, meaning, and depth, searched for the Sacred inside the profane, longed to define myself, mark my place, find the way to be blessed by the Gods of abundance...*then* I'll be happy and content. I know, deep down, the search is endless, but it's what I do, what I've always done, and everyone I know has been riding the same train, so I've slid one coin after another into the slot, unawares there's no matanoia, no unicorns, no rainbow in the end, no golden jackpot. It's time to face my deepest fear: to end the search, to simply let go and trust.

I smile, gazing at the wrapper. All the Gurus, teachers, and books on Self- help, and my deepest revelation's printed on some snot-nosed kid's candy wrapper.

The city of Boston grows small below as my plane lifts into the clouds; I'm on the beginning of a thirty-three hour stretch back to Denpasar after a month long sojourn in the States with Mom. Her image arises; posing before me, a dress dangling from each hand- which one to wear for the dance? I watched her while she sweetly hummed into the mirror and ran a brush through her silver hair. I'd never seen her so happy and contented.

I settle into my seat, snuggle into a blanket and close my eyes.

When mom and I drove through maple New England roads, where Brian and I once so often traveled, my heart ached, missing his friendship and company. He's been married for over a year now.

Stephen and Sarah remain dear friends. The last time I saw Stephen, he held me ethereally in my dreams, in the deepest love and adoration. At present they are both with other partners and lovingly separated.

As for Father Ron, his 'Temple' in Santa Fe was closed after a member of a police Swat team arrested an employee that was indicted as part of a major prostitution ring bust. Was it meaningless chance, or the Gods of Karma and Magic?

My relationship with Ron forced me to learn how to stand on my own, respect my intuition and needs, and find dignity and self-respect. I discovered that, although boundaries may best become defined by stepping over them, true freedom can only be found within their safe and well-developed confines. I will forever be grateful for the experiences that taught me this.

It is said in Tantric philosophy that life is contradiction. We live in a world of duality, light/dark, good/evil, male/female, observing ourselves as separate from one another. Yet duality is Maya, the illusion: The miraculous dance of Spirit, the veil of Divine Oneness. We're manifest as a perfect combination of flesh and Spirit, God consciousness animating mortal bodies. God split into two for the purpose of observing Self: God observing God. You cannot observe something without an observer, and the observed can only be seen and known from its opposition, which in essence, is one and the same. You cannot know wet unless you experience dry, fullness without empty, wealth from poverty, joy from pain, or right, without wrong. You cannot know Divinity without seeing what Divinity is not; yet can said latter exist? Maya is the dance and play of Divine paradox.

Art, love, music, and passion...the variance of brilliant hearts and minds; from where would any of it arise if not for something to stand for or against? Ask Eve in her garden; if the world were completely safe, clean, perfect... what then would we look towards?

Can truth, beauty, and all that is Sacred, be found without knowing their opposites?

Shall we shoot the messengers who help us to discover this?

At forty years old, and with the completion of this book, I look upon my life with a deep sense of meaning and purpose. The metamorphosis, like that of a butterfly, was nothing thought out or planned, arriving hardly noticed, perhaps sneaking in whilst I slept like a burglar in the night: a gentle calming, an understanding, more of the body than of the mind.

I've come to know, from the depths of my Soul, there is no longer anything to pursue, nothing I must find 'out there' to complete me.

Everything I've needed, even in the darkest of nights, has always been here and with me.

We are all so vulnerably precious and human, and in the same breath, divine. The two are never separate, always one within our fathers, mothers, teachers, enemies, friends, lovers...and most of all, ourselves.

From roots that grow deep down into the mud...the lotus ascends to receive the light of the sun.

This is my experience.

No Mud, No Lotus.

About the Author

Maya is an Acharya, which means a person who is educated through the depths of intensive personal experience. At thirty three, after twelve years of life threatening addictions, Maya began a radical journey into Self healing through diving deeply into the Tantras: first, the red or left hand path, via Tantra and Sacred Sex of the West, which landed her in a controversial documentary film about Tantra. After several years of working as a Tantric practitioner, she denounced the practice and took refuge into White Tantra, the right hand path, through the eastern Sikh tradition of Kundalini yoga. Her experiences naturally led her to advocate the path of balance, or 'The Middle Way.' Maya teaches Kundalini Yoga, Personal Empowerment and Integral Self Development. She lives in Ubud, Bali.

www.ramamaya.com

FB: "No Mud, No Lotus"